INSTANT EXPERT

M

W9-BIS-515

COLLE
TEAPOTS

Leah Rousmaniere

HOUSE OF COLLECTIBLES
NEW YORK

CONTENTS

For my mother-in-law, Jessie Rousmaniere,
with whom I've shared many a
companionable cup of tea, with love

INTRODUCTION

Everyone has a teapot story.

I found that out when I undertook the writing of this book; everyone I knew wanted to tell me one. Some individuals, warming to the topic, told several. People wrote me E-mails about their teapots, their mothers' teapots, their aunts' teapots. One friend wrote feelingly about a teapot someone had given him while he was stationed in England with the U.S. Army during the 1960s. He still has it, along with several others he has since collected along the way. Another friend, at the moment living in Hong Kong, put me on to the Flagstaff House Museum of Tea Ware (a branch of the Hong Kong Museum of Art), and its sizable collection of teapots, including one that dates from 1513. Yet another friend just happened to know the woman who had recently curated the Chinese export porcelain exhibit at the Metropolitan Museum of Art. Yet another—a very dear friend in her eighties—spontaneously burst into the old playground song, "I'm a Little Teapot."

All this just because I said, "I'm writing a book on collecting teapots."

What is it about teapots, anyway? Not only did everyone to whom I mentioned my book have a teapot story to tell me, but he or she also knew someone who collected teapots. Within what seemed like minutes I had a vast compendium of phone numbers and E-mail addresses. Clearly, I realized immediately, teapot collectors are a very friendly group.

So there's no reason for you to feel intimidated if you're just starting out. Perhaps you have a few teapots by accident—people have given them to you over the years, or you've picked up one here and there, as I did when I first started out—and you'd like to know a little something more about them. Perhaps your Great Uncle Ferdinand has just left you an attic full of them, and you're at a loss as to what to do. Maybe you're having wistful thoughts about your childhood, in which tea and teapots loomed large in the comfort department. Or maybe you just wish you had had a childhood in which tea and teapots loomed large.

No reason you can't collect a few and start now.

Teapots are whimsical. Teapots are fun. Teapots rise up from the nether age of consciousness. Can you remember a time when you didn't know what one was? How old were you when you first learned "I'm a little teapot / short and stout"? Certainly before you were old enough to actually drink tea on any kind of a regular basis. Perhaps you had a toy tea set as a child, to serve tea to your bears and dolls. I know I did.

Or, at least, I think I know I did.

Ponder that for a moment: I may or may not have had a toy tea set, yet I distinctly remember serving tea to my bears and dolls . . . Or do I? Perhaps I only saw the Norman Rockwell magazine cover. If there even *was* a Norman Rockwell magazine cover. My memory may be faulty there, too.

Because teapots are iconic. There's a collective consciousness about them. They're archetypal; they touch us in the bottom of our souls. They represent something, although we may be at pains to articulate exactly what that something may be. Never mind that most of us grew up in households where the adults drank coffee. In a country where the adults predominantly drank coffee. In a country whose founding fathers and mothers, in fact, filled Boston Harbor with tea rather than pay the hated tax—thus ensuring that we became a nation of coffee drinkers.

Show me a teapot, and I am comforted.

And I'm not the only one. More people collect teapots than collect anything else, for a variety of reasons

"The essence varies from person to person," ceramics gallery owner Garth Clark explained a few years ago to Joyce Lovelace, writing for *American Craft Magazine*. "Some [collectors] have an interest in the culture of tea, and the teapot is an icon for that. Or they fall in love with the vitality and jauntiness of the form. Visually, it's very arresting and interesting. And it's lively—it moves. It also allows for all kinds of games with anthropomorphism—legs, arms, sexual organs. Beautifully resolved, it can be the most expressive object a potter can make."

Teapots also have a sense of humor. As Edward Bramah points out in his excellent *Novelty Teapots: Five Hundred Years of Art and Design*, tea and coffee became popular drinks in Europe at about the same time, in the mid-17th century. Both had to be brewed, both were drunk hot, and both were served in pots. But from the outset, strange shapes and decoration were confined almost completely to teapots. "Coffee has never been a laughing matter," Bramah muses, "but this does not explain why tea should have attracted to itself so much humour over the last three hundred years."

Or why, almost as soon as tea and teapots arrived in Europe, European potters began turning out not only teapots in which to brew tea, but also teapots that were too delicate and too complicated to brew tea—teapots meant only for display, to be set out in china cabinets and admired. Hardly had German potter Johann Böttger figured out how to make hard-paste porcelain (an industrial secret carefully guarded by the Chinese), than the newly founded Meissen company began turning out the first novelty teapots.

Exciting but impractical, these teapots never poured particularly well, but no one seemed to care. Beautiful to behold, intricate, exquisitely formed and decorated, these teapots transcended function and delighted their new owners, who set them lovingly and proudly on a shelf—and went on brewing tea in their Chinese export porcelain or redware teapots.

Tea was first drunk in England and Europe in the first half of the 17th century; the earliest recorded reference to tea in English was made by Richard Wickham of the East India Company in 1615, in a letter to a colleague in Macao asking him to send him some. By 1658 there was enough interest in the product for the owner of the Sultaness-head, a London "Cophee-house," to place an ad in the *Mercurius Politicus* introducing "That Excellent, and by all Physitians approved, China Drink, called by the Chineans, Tcha, by other Nations Tay, alias Tee." Two years later, at least one London proprietor was selling tea in leaf form for 15 shillings per pound.

The earliest surviving example of a ceramic European teapot was made between 1670 and 1680 by Ary de Milde in the Dutch town of Delft. Less than 50 years later, there were European teapot collectors. And factories making teapots for them to collect. François Boucher, the most fashionable French painter of his day, was one of the earliest collectors of teapots. He was born in 1703. Boucher, it turns out, collected just about anything, including porcelains, minerals, shells, precious stones, lacquerwork, weapons, you name it. After he died in 1770, it took his widow three years to liquidate and divide his estate—including, presumably, the teapot collection, estimated by some historians to have included 250 pots. It is tempting to imagine Madame Boucher, faced with the lot, standing there scratching her head. Wondering how to find out more about teapots. What kind of dealer might buy or sell them. Whether or not some other teapot collector out there might be interested in acquiring the entire collection. A particularly fanciful person might even imagine for a moment that Madame Boucher considered keeping the teapots and becoming a teapot collector herself. If so, more questions would have presented themselves: What to collect? Why to collect it? How and where to start?

Perhaps you are pondering these very questions.

Dear Reader, *Instant Expert: Collecting Teapots* is the book for you.

1

WHAT IS AN INSTANT EXPERT?

An instant expert is someone who knows how to ask questions, what questions to ask, how to listen to the answers to those questions, how to organize what he or she finds out—and how to then ask more questions, following up on the new information.

Anyone can become an instant expert. It doesn't mean you'll be a *real* expert like someone who has been selling antiques for twenty years, or who has a Ph.D. in Chinese export porcelain. But make your way through this book, and I guarantee you'll know enough—and be comfortable enough—to talk to a real expert.

Let's say you have a particular teapot that has come into your possession. You want to know more. How and where to start?

Questions to Ask about Your Teapot
Teapot or Kettle?
What you think is a teapot may be a kettle and vice-versa. A kettle is a vessel for boiling or cooking and can withstand that kind of heat. A teapot is for brewing tea. There is a type of cast-iron teapot, usually made in China or Japan although some are now made in the United States, that can be used as a kettle to boil water or as a teapot to brew tea. Many modern versions of these teakettle-teapots (often called by their Japanese name, *tetsubin*) come with a stainless mesh infuser for brewing loose tea. But generally, a kettle is a kettle.

If your kettle has a matching metal stand, it may be a "tipping kettle." Wrought-iron, brass, and copper tea kettles with stands were popular at the turn of the 20th century. Some models allowed the server to pour by tipping, without actually hefting the pot; hence the name. Others provided a space underneath for a heat source (a forerunner of the modern Sterno can). These kettles would presumably be used to pour hot water into teapots.

Ceramic teapots with overhead handles are often called "kettles." A more exact usage of terminology would be "kettle-shape."

Metal or Ceramic?
You should be able to tell by looking at your teapot whether it's metal or ceramic. An earthenware teapot decorated with platinum lustre might look like silver on first glance; an agateware teapot like real agate; or a Wedgwood basalt stoneware teapot with its deep, brown-black color like your mother's old cast-iron frying pan—but on careful examination, you will see that these are all actually ceramic teapots.

Many of us remember our mother's or grandmother's silver tea set, proudly and lovingly displayed on the dining-room sideboard or behind glass doors in the china cabinet. In colonial times pewter was the poor man's silver, although much of it on this side of the Atlantic was

Hall Rhythm teapot. Marked on the bottom "Hall, made in USA, 1400." While somewhat unconventionally or stylistically shaped, this is a functional teapot designed to brew tea. Teapot courtesy Miriam Novalle, T Salon & T Emporium.

melted down for ordnance during the Revolutionary War. In recent years, pewter has become popular again. There are also brass and copper teapots.

Functional or Novelty?

A teapot that is designed to brew tea is considered functional. There are, however, teapots no one would ever dream of using to make tea, and teapots you couldn't use to make tea even if you wanted to. These are novelty teapots, and they've been around almost from the beginning of tea drinking in Europe.

It may seem strange that anyone would want to make—or buy—a teapot that can't be used to brew tea, but, as Leslie Ferrin (host of several teapot shows each year at the Ferrin Gallery in Northampton, Massachusetts) says, "The art of collecting is by nature subjective, and the subjectiveness of the teapot is endless." Teapots inspire strong archetypal associations that have nothing to do with tea brewing or drinking. Many ceramics artists, artists working in other media, and collectors are fascinated by the teapot form.

"I like the tension between the tradition of the teapot and its most unlikely interpretations," Joan Takayama-Ogawa, a Los Angeles ceramist, told Joyce Lovelace for her article in *American Craft Magazine*. Said North Carolina potter Michael Sherrill in the same article, "My

Cardew gnome mobile market teapot. A modern novelty teapot. Technically, you *could* brew tea in it, but you probably wouldn't. Available at this writing for $220.00 at www.abitofbritain.com.

teapots are in no way functional. I'm not interested in whether it pours or not, but does it work visually?" Other artists and collectors speak in terms of the "representational teapot," the teapot as "the most iconic of ceramic symbols," or the teapot as "metaphor for the body, for life."

Some novelty teapots can be used to brew tea—at least theoretically. Others are strictly sculptural. These lofty, one-of-a-kind teapots can "start at $1,000.00 for emerging artists, range from $2,000.00 to $10,000.00 for more established artists, and run over $20,000.00 for seminal works from important artists of the '60s and early '70s," according to Lynda McDaniel, writing recently for *American Style Magazine*. Even more recently, there was an article in the *New York Times* by Chee Pearlman, "From Alessi, a Second Chance to Buy a $50,000 Teapot." It is doubtful anyone would use such pots to brew tea, even if they are 100 percent functional.

Does It Say Anything on the Bottom?

In a perfect world, every piece of pottery or porcelain that was ever produced would carry a manufacturer's mark indicating the date and place of manufacture, the name of the potter, the name of the company, and the name of the pattern or design. Unfortunately, this is not a perfect world. Some modern teapots do provide a great deal of information (for example, my Minton teapot, on the bottom of which is stamped, "B-1451/Haddon Hall/

Minton/founded 1793/Bone China/ made in England/designed by John Wadsworth"). But many teapots have no marks whatsoever. And, unfortunately, some teapots have marks that are unreliable. But don't despair. Whatever your teapot does or doesn't say on the bottom, there are ways to find out more.

Minton fluted Fife shape teapot. Marked on bottom: "B-1451 / Haddon Hall / Minton / founded 1763 / Bone China / made in England / designed by John Wadsworth." A teapot collector's dream mark; all marks should be so fulsomely informative. Inspired by the needlework tapestries hanging at Haddon Hall, Derbyshire, England, this is the most popular Minton pattern of all time. Wadsworth designed the collection in 1948, but the teapot shape is turn of the 20th century. Note especially the "dripless" spout, a popular innovation alleged to pour without dripping.

Perhaps not in five minutes, however. As Lois Lehner points out in her *Lehner's Encyclopedia of U.S. Marks on Pottery, Porcelain, and Clay*, "There are over 1,900 companies, potters, potteries with over 8,000 marks, logos, symbols etc. divided about equally among the old folk potters, studio potters, dinnerware manufacturers, selling agencies or distributors, decorative or art pottery, decorators, decorating companies and decorative tile."

And that's just in the United States; Lehner doesn't include marks made by companies, potters, and potteries in other countries. Moreover, Lehner continues, "As monumental as the mound of written material (about ceramic marks) is now, we need at least that much more work before we will begin to conquer the subject." This from a woman whose book is the size of the Manhattan Yellow Pages, and who confesses that it took her eight years to compile the information in it, and before that an additional fifteen years of researching potteries for various other books she has written.

So we won't have room to do the subject of ceramics marks justice here. But here are the basics:

Pottery Marks

The word *mark* is loosely employed to designate anything used by a potter or company to identify a product. A mark can be:

stamped on with ink (*backstamp*)

scratched into the clay by hand (*incised mark*)

pressed into the clay (*impressed mark*)

raised in the clay (*raised mark*)

painted on, either under or over the glaze (*painted mark*)

stuck on (*paper label*)

Some ceramic-marking methods are less felicitous than others, as will become immediately apparent when you scrutinize the half-obliterated mark on the bottom of a teapot left you by dear Uncle Ferdinand. Backstamps can sometimes wear off. Impressed and raised marks made in the mold may or may not show up on the finished piece. Incised marks scratched into the clay may be for all practical purposes illegible. As for those stuck-on paper labels, they were probably removed at first opportunity by the teapot's original owner.

As John Ramsay pointed out many years ago in his excellent article, "Marks of China and Pottery" in the periodical *Hobbies*, marks are "often omitted, occasionally impossible to identify from our present data, and not infrequently misleading." Some are downright forgeries dating back years and years—Meissen, for example, sued a Dresden porcelain factory as early as the 18th century to get the Dresden firm to stop marking its wares *Meissen*. Also in the 1700s, Josiah Wedgwood defended his marks and reputation in court against unscrupulous

imitators. The occasional American manufacturer has been known to mark its wares with designs ambiguous enough to masquerade as English or European, hence a proliferation of lions, unicorns, shield marks, knots, and garters. Other marks can fall into the extremely gray area of "homage," particularly those made by Chinese potters hoping to honor illustrious master potters of yesteryear.

Poole Pottery teapot, ca. 1990s. Marked on the bottom, "Hand Painted, Microwave, Dishwasher & Freezer Safe, Poole Pottery, England," this is a typical, modern teabag-teapot: no strainer at the base of the spout. The "microwave safe" dates it 1970s and thereafter.

That said, most if not all marks are accurate and believable; a great deal about a teapot's origin can often be learned from any marks on it, and the only problem may be tracking down the mark. For those marks not readily decipherable, including numbers, squiggles, scribbles, and what-have-you, I refer you to the several books on marks listed in the Bibliography. Ralph and Terry Kovel's books can be particularly helpful. Meanwhile, here are some helpful hints about some of the more common (modern) marks:

Oven Proof
If your teapot is marked "oven proof," it was manufactured after 1933.

Dishwasher Proof
If it's marked "dishwasher proof," it postdates 1955.

Microwave Safe
If it is marked "microwave safe," it was manufactured in or after 1970.

Bone China
Bone china was developed around 1800, but the words *bone china* did not appear as a mark until about 1915.

Country Name

The McKinley Tariff of 1891 required that any items imported into the United States have the country of origin marked on them. In some cases, companies and potters were already putting the country of origin on their wares before 1891; in others, companies failed to comply, the marks have worn off, or the paper labels have since been removed. Country names can be a clue to date of manufacture; if a teapot is marked "Made in Russia," for example, the piece would be dated before 1917 or after 1991. "Made in Occupied Japan" indicates a date of manufacture between September 1945 and April 1952, when Japan resumed full sovereignty.

Date

A caveat regarding any date you may find on the bottom of your teapot: most often it is the date the company was founded, not the date the teapot was manufactured. Be wary, too, of any dates included in the decoration; a piece marked "1776," for example, most likely was produced to mark the Bicentennial in 1976.

Copyright Symbol (©)

The earliest the Kovels have seen a © mark is 1914.

Copyright

The earliest the Kovels have seen the entire word written out as part of the mark is 1892.

Chinese Characters

As noted above, Chinese potters are fond of rendering homage. Rather than mark their wares with their own names or factories, some prefer to honor glorious dynastic reigns from a few centuries ago, or express a sentiment that while interesting neither dates your teapot nor helps determine its origin. There is a book on Chinese porcelain marks for people who can't read Chinese, compiled by London expert Gerald Davidson. One mark in Davidson's book translates "Studio for the Preservation of Awkwardness," while another reads "Studio Where I Want to Hear My Faults." Other marks like "Made During the Yuanfeng Reign of the Great Song Dynasty" would date manufacture of your teapot long before brewing tea became commonplace, even in China (the Song or Sung dynasty was ca. 960–1279 C.E.). If you want to know what your teapot's Chinese inscription says, Davidson's book is the place to look.

Chinese Yixing (redware) teapots often have the stamp or "chop" of the potter. But again, the mark may honor an illustrious potter of yesteryear.

Manufacturer Name
If the name of the manufacturer, pottery, or potter is marked on your teapot, you're ahead of the game. Company Web sites often contain a wealth of information that will help you learn more, including contact phone numbers, E-mail addresses, and useful links. Many companies will answer questions and help you identify your teapot.

Don't shy away from commercial Web sites; they often have photos that can identify types of pottery, glazes, patterns, or teapot shapes. A Google Internet search for "Wedgwood teapot," for example, produced 298 results at this writing, and a visit to eBay and the same search got nine hits. Check the Index and Bibliography in this book to see what information I have to offer on various companies and potteries, then widen your search.

Gaynor Laight's *www.crackedchina.co.uk* offers a link to an excellent Web site with pages and pages on ceramic marks (more on Internet searches later). She also has links to many company Web sites. In the past, Laight has even been willing, from time to time, to post photos of ceramic items submitted by stumped owners in the hope that other Web site visitors can identify them.

Public libraries are wonderful resources; often the place to start when researching your teapot mark is the card or online catalog at your local library. Even if you live in Po-dunk, Timbuktu, your local librarian may be able to produce the most seemingly-unattainable books on interlibrary loan. The Web site *www.abebooks.com* offers an astonishing service; if they don't have the book you're looking for, they'll prompt you with "Find it at a local library;" click on that, and the OCLC WorldCat page opens. (OCLC is the world's largest bibliographic database built by the world's libraries.) Both Borders and Barnes & Noble have books on ceramic marks; they may prefer to sell them to you, but they won't mind if you sit on the floor and read them instead.

Don't give up if the company name scrawled on the bottom of your teapot is so obscure no one seems to have heard of it. Flip through some of the books on marks listed in the Bibliography. Even if you don't find what you're looking for now, as you learn and become more knowledgeable, you may discover that the proverbial lightbulb goes on over your head another day.

If there are no marks on the bottom of your teapot, closely examine it to make sure there are no marks anywhere. Occasionally, teapots are marked under the lid. Chinese and Japanese teapots may be marked just under the handle.

And if your teapot has no marks whatsoever . . . perhaps it's old enough to predate the use of marks, although it may be just one of the thousands of ceramics made but not marked and marketed in the late 19th century and 20th century. Consider it a challenge.

As Geoffrey Godden reminds readers in his introduction to Philip Miller's and Michael Berthoud's *An Anthology of British Teapots*, "a still unidentified pot may well be the most noteworthy in a collection and indeed many of the teapots shown [in the *Anthology*] were purchased by Philip Miller and other students just because they were unidentified and presented a problem. Many such problems remain!"

Pottery or Porcelain?

I hope your teapot will have said on the bottom what it is. Even if it didn't, now is a good time to discuss the various kinds of ceramics.

Ceramics is a large field. Even dealers can't identify all the different kinds, although they can recognize immediately whatever it is they specialize in, and hazard an educated guess about the rest. Certainly they can tell the difference between pottery and porcelain. After a while, you'll be able to tell the difference, too. But you will have to start looking at pottery and porcelain items to develop an eye.

Luckily, you already own a large collection of ceramic ware: your dishes. I'm going to bet that your everyday stuff is probably pottery and that your good stuff—wedding presents or inherited items—may be porcelain.

Experts will tell you that porcelain has a certain "ring" to it—if you tap a porcelain teapot and a pottery teapot, you'll be able to hear the difference. Maybe. I tapped every piece of ceramic in my apartment to see if this was true, and you might want to conduct the same experiment. While the Minton bone-china teapot did have a very noticeable ring, my Lenox Jefferson fine-china dinner plates did not. I did notice that the sound of my everyday dishes—which I'm sure are pottery, even though they don't say so—was more of a thud than a ring.

Another test for porcelain is its translucence. Hold your teapot up to the light. Can you sort of see through the bottom of it? Hold up your good dinner plates while you're at it. I could see through my Lenox plates, even if they didn't ring. However, just because it's porcelain doesn't mean you'll be able to see through it. Some types of porcelain are heavier than others. A heavy porcelain baking dish in my possession, for example. To say nothing of bathtubs and toilets. (You forgot those were porcelain, didn't you? Just goes to show: you know more than you think.)

Conversely, just because you can sort of see through it doesn't mean it's porcelain; witness the Lenox dinner plates. A definition of porcelain offered at www.Lenox.com was not helpful: "A hard, translucent clayware that differs slightly from china in ingredients and manufacturing; the terms ('china' and 'porcelain') can be used interchangeably." So is fine china porcelain or not? I asked the Lenox people about my dinner plates: not porcelain, it turned out, but fine china—which explains why they don't ring.

But then why use the terms "china" and "porcelain" interchangeably?

Here I hazard my own conjecture (not to be attributed to the people at Lenox):

Because porcelain originally came from China and the Chinese were the only ones who knew how to make it, the stuff came to be called "china." That word *china* was used later to describe porcelain made in Europe, perhaps much in the way *Xerox* is used today even when making copies on, say, a Canon copier—not technically "Xeroxing." Some years after the Europeans figured out how to make their own porcelain, Americans produced a similar hard, translucent ceramic. At the time, American manufacturers hoped to supplant Chinese, British, German, and French porcelain imports. They may also have hoped that potential buyers wouldn't notice that their new product wasn't exactly "real" porcelain. Not the first ambiguous ad campaign in history; cry "havoc" and let slip the dogs of confusion. (In the American manufacturers' favor, what came to be called "fine china" was fine enough to see through; it just didn't ring.)

The ambiguity of ceramics terminology, unfortunately, does not stop with "fine china."

Basically, all ceramics are pottery. Pottery is anything made out of clay that has been baked, including bricks that have been baked in the sun, like the Pueblo Indians used to make their adobe dwellings. Any coarse clay can be baked at low temperatures to make pottery. Stoneware is a more sophisticated kind of pottery made from a mix of clay with fewer impurities, and fired at higher temperatures. Except that the term *pottery* is often used to mean *only* coarser-clay items fired at lower temperatures, as opposed to *stoneware*, which are purer-clay items fired at higher temperatures. You begin to appreciate the problem: *stoneware* is and is not *pottery*. Porcelain is technically a kind of pottery—the most pure kaolin clay fired at the highest temperatures. Except that when experts say porcelain, they mean *not* pottery.

Go ahead: say "Huh?" I did. Here's the crux of the matter: Some experts divide ceramics into two categories: pottery and porcelain. That group considers stoneware to be a type of pottery. Other experts divide ceramics into three categories: pottery, stoneware, and porcelain. The three-category system makes more sense to me, given the easy-to-remember distinctions between pottery, stoneware, and porcelain:

Pottery: made from a coarser grade of clay that is fired at lower temperatures.

McCoy pottery teapot, ca. 1930s. Marked on bottom, "McCoy." Hand-crafted. Teapot courtesy Miriam Novalle, T Salon & T Emporium.

Stoneware: made from clay with fewer impurities than that used for pottery, fired at higher temperatures.

Porcelain: made from the purest white kaolin clay, fired at the highest temperatures.

Since the majority opinion seems to be in favor of two categories, pottery vs. porcelain, we'll desist arguing semantics and go with the flow. (Stoneware, I dub thee Pottery.)

There are many different types of pottery, which, by the way, is also called *earthenware*. Those beautiful black-and-orange-pottery Greek vases you see in museums the world over? Those are *redware*. Mexican pottery is also considered a kind of redware. *Creamware* is a cream-colored pottery developed by Josiah Wedgwood in the mid-18th century; it's also called *Queensware*, because Queen Charlotte (wife of King George III) liked it and ordered a huge service for the palace. *Yellowware* is a type of pottery used to make heavy, durable kitchenware; your grandmother may have had yellowware mixing bowls.

Majolica, *faience*, and *delft*, considered by many experts to be the same thing (majolica being the Italian, faience the French, and delft the Dutch names for it, respectively), are a kind of pottery made of coarse clay and covered with an opaque tin-oxide glaze; majolica and faience in particular are known for their bright, festive colors. (*Majolica* is pronounced either "meh-JO-lick-a" or "may-YO-lick-a;" *faience* is pronounced "fay-AHNS," swallowing the *N* the way the French do.)

According to Paul Atterbury, author of *The History of Porcelain*, the modern definition of porcelain is quite precise: it is hard, translucent, and resonant (it "rings"), and it is composed of two specific ingredients. These are *kaolin*, a pure white clay, and *petuntse*, a type of feldspar rock. "Chemically," Atterbury writes, "kaolin is aluminium silicate and petuntse is aluminium and potassium silicate. Physically, they behave like flour and fat in pastry; mixed together in the correct proportions they combine to give a workable paste which is hardened by heat—in the case of porcelain, intense heat." The high heat (at least 1,450 degrees Centigrade or 2,640 degrees Fahrenheit) is what makes the finished porcelain piece hard and strong.

Bone china—not to be confused with fine china—is made from a mix of kaolin clay and animal-bone ash; unlike fine china, it is considered porcelain.

There is something called *soft-paste* porcelain, which is what the Europeans made before they figured out how to make *real* or *hard-paste* porcelain in the early 18th century. True soft-paste porcelain is no longer made, although some experts consider all American porcelain by strict definition to be soft-paste. We'll talk more about it in Chapter 3.

But back to your teapot: Can you hazard a guess whether it's pottery or porcelain? Is it resonant—does it ring when you tap it? Is it translucent—can you sort of see through it? If so, it's porcelain. If not, it's pottery. If it doesn't ring, but you can sort of see through it, it's possibly porcelain, but more likely fine china.

What Condition Is It In?

Ceramic teapots, while durable, do break or become damaged. A rare teapot may be rare in fact because most others like it have broken over the years. Basically, a teapot that is in excellent condition has no repairs, cracks, chips, or crazing. Crazing is a network of fine lines, usually caused by extremes of heat or cold—leaving a teapot in the attic or unheated garage for years on end, say, or by putting a non-dishwasher-safe item in the dishwasher. Technically, crazing is caused by the clay body and glaze reacting differently to changes in temperature and environment; the body goes one way and the glaze goes the other.

If you visit antiques shops and fairs—which you should start doing, by the way, if you want to see teapots and prices and different kinds of pottery and porcelain face-to-face—you will soon notice that scrupulous dealers note any kind of repair, chip, or crack on the price tag, or they will point out problems to you when you inquire about the item. (Dealers who don't should make you nervous. Remember: The rule is Buyer Beware, not Seller Beware.) Obviously, a little chip on the inside rim of the lid that you can't see when the lid is in place will devalue the piece less than a nicked handle or spout. Tea stains may or may not be considered a drawback, especially if they are inside (and unseen) only; but a dealer should call your attention to them if present.

An item in less than pristine condition may still be worth something. I am the proud owner of a World War II–era "War-Against-Hitlerism" teapot with a broken lid (expertly repaired), considerable tea stains inside, and a small amount of crazing. I care not a whit about any of these flaws. Had the teapot been in excellent condition, I probably would not have been able to afford it; instead, the dealer, offering it for sale "as is," gave me what I considered an excellent buy.

There's a category of antique teapots and tea caddies called "Make-Do's." Teresa Kurau, of Historical China in

War Against Hitlerism, earthenware, ca. 1939–1945. Banners read: "This Souvenir Teapot was made for DYSON & HORSFALL of PRESTON to replace Aluminium Stocks taken over for ALLIED ARMAMENTS, 1939"; "THAT RIGHT SHALL PREVAIL"; and "LIBERTY and FREEDOM." Marked on bottom "DUCAL WARE" and "MADE IN ENGLAND"; the rest of the stamp is illegible. Tea stains; crazing; part of inside flange of lid broken away (not visible when lid is in place); visibly repaired lid. $95.00 "as is" in the 1990s.

Lampeter, Pennsylvania, showed me an 18th-century Chinese-export-porcelain Make-Do teapot with a silver spout; the original spout had broken off and was replaced with a silver one. Sometimes a teapot's or tea caddy's lid has broken and been replaced in the same way. Some collectors specialize in Make-Do's.

For the most part, your teapot must be in excellent condition to fetch a good price. It must have its original lid; a teapot without a lid, or with a mismatched replacement lid (even if it's a great fit) is virtually worthless, unless it's a Make-Do like Kurau's.

Take a moment to closely examine your teapot for any repairs, cracks, chips, or crazing. Run your hands over it, then take off the lid and look inside. If there are any flaws (including tea stains), note them. If you aspire to serious collecting, now may be the time to develop the habit of noting things in writing. Write on a slip of paper the date the teapot came into your possession; where it came from; if you bought it, how much you paid for it and anything the dealer might have told you about it; and any flaws you may notice. Use decent-quality paper and indelible ink. Put the slip of paper into the pot. As you learn more about your teapot, you can add more slips of paper. That way, a hundred years from now, your great-grandchildren won't be scratching their heads like Madame Boucher.

Is There a Strainer at the Bottom of the Spout?

A strainer inside at the bottom of your teapot's spout can help date your pot. As Edward Bramah explains in *Novelty Teapots: Five Hundred Years of Art and Design*, all the teapots that have survived from the 1700s and most from the 1800s were made to brew Chinese tea, which was a very different tea from what we drink today. Chinese tea was rolled by hand, and the leaf that unfurled in the pot was quite large; some leaves were as large as postage stamps.

"The strainer inside many old teapots at the base of the spout had to have quite large holes to allow the tea to escape between the tea leaves" when poured, Bramah writes. Contrast that to the modern-day teapot, made to brew tea in bags. With the introduction of instant coffee to the British market in the mid 1950s, drinkers of both coffee and tea became impatient; people were no longer willing to wait a few minutes for large-leaf tea to unfurl and brew. "Changes were made in the production of much of the tea produced in northeast India and Africa so that the shape of the tea leaf in the traditional sense all but disappeared," Bramah continues. "From such faster-brewing tea it was but one small step to the teabag." From about the mid 1970s on, many teapot manufacturers began to dispense with the strainer. The tea-bag teapot was born.

If your teapot has no strainer at the base of the spout, it's probably not much older than the 1970s. (Unless your teapot seems old enough to predate strainers at the base of the spout, which first came into use in the early 18th century, in which case you may have a museum piece on your hands.)

Jane Bennett, the teaware assistant at Norwich Castle Museum and Art Gallery in England (which has the largest collection of British ceramic teapots in the world), offers another interesting fact about strainers at the base of the spout: In the latter part of the 19th century, different British factories were identifiable by the number of holes in the strainer. Moreover, according to Bennett, "certain factories would make different patterns" of holes. "People come a long way just to look at one or two teapots in our collection," she says, "simply to look at the strainer and count holes in the pattern."

While a trip to England to identify your teapot may be neither your inclination nor within your budget, Jane Bennett's knowledge of strainers is something to keep in mind for future reference if all else fails.

Is It Figural?

A figural teapot is a pot in the shape of an animal, person, house, vegetable, fruit, automobile, birthday cake, piano . . . . You get the idea: It is shaped like just about anything. They can be functional, nonfunctional, or somewhere in between.

A teapot in the shape of something is not a new idea; in China and Japan, figural teapots have been made for centuries. There are some very old figural Yixing (Chinese redware) teapots in the collection at the Flagstaff Museum of Teaware in Hong Kong. Bundles of bamboo were a popular motif, as were dragons and various Buddhist persons of note. Teapots in these shapes made their way to England and continental Europe as early as the 17th century, where they were soon copied by potters producing claywares for the local markets. Although popular as whimsical pieces, figural teapots never quite made it as far as the formal tea table; when serving tea socially, the lady of the house needed something a little more traditional.

Nonetheless, figural teapots were collected then as now. Some enthusiasts specialize in a particular type of figural: monkey teapots, say, or cottage teapots. Others collect teapots made by one particular designer—Paul Cardew, for example, whose magnificently whimsical novelties often find their way even into the hands of people who don't normally collect teapots. There are pottery figurals and porcelain figurals, old figurals and new figurals—in short, there is no limit to the number of figural teapots out there just waiting for collectors to collect them. See the Index for specific examples.

Camel figural teapot. Pottery, marked on the bottom "Made in Japan," with an internal six-hole strainer at the base of the spout. My stepson and daughter-in-law, graduates of Connecticut College, where the mascot is a camel, like it for no other reason than that. Price in the mid-1990s: $35.00.

What Shape Is It?

If your teapot isn't a figural, but is functional and designed to brew tea, chances are it will fall into a specific teapot-shape category. You will learn to recognize shapes as time goes on, by visiting antiques shops and fairs, and by viewing photos of teapots online and in books.

There are more teapot shapes than we can discuss here. The standard book on shapes is Philip Miller's and Michael Berthoud's excellent compendium, *An Anthology of British Teapots*, which contains 2,268 black-and-white examples of teapots arranged in 16 sections by shape, date, maker, etc., covering the years ca. 1710–1983. A chart of some American teapot shapes has been posted by collectors of Hall China at *www.inter-services.com/HallChina/idcharts.html* and is worth a look.

The older your teapot, and the more traditional, the more likely it is to fit a particular named shape. By far the most common modern shape is the Brown Betty (see photo on page (89). See the Index under "shapes" for more examples.

What's It Worth?

Anyone who watches *Antiques Roadshow* is familiar with the drill:

You proffer your item. The expert tells you about it. Only last does the expert get around to mentioning price. You

Commode-shape teapot. Also called "old silver shape." Probably porcelain, probably 19th century; teapot detectives are on the case. Very visible repairs. Teapot courtesy David Wood.

may squirm in your chair, various emotions may play across your face, your entire body language may telepathically convey to both expert and television audience that the only thing you're REALLY interested in is WHAT'S IT WORTH?!?—yet still the expert resolutely plods on, telling you ABOUT the item and leaving the possible price to last.

Welcome to Dealer-Expert Etiquette 101. The experts on *Antiques Roadshow* graciously, time after time, and despite any boorish price-fixation on the part of the profferer of the item, demonstrate the correct profferer/dealer-expert interaction: you ask about the item. The dealer tells you about it. Only last, and if at all possible with a slight moue of afterthought, is price mentioned.

It's a lesson worth learning. While writing this book, I called the proprietor of an antiques shop specializing in American pottery, and asked him to help with my project. I was at the early stages of the project, and I might not have explained my intent clearly enough, when suddenly the dealer yelled, "Is this another one of those infernal price guides?" Without waiting for an answer, he launched into a 10-minute rant about ill-mannered people coming into his shop, proffering whatever, and asking, "What's it worth?" without any other prelude. (Clearly I had pushed a button with this man.) Desperate to recover the interview, I finally said, "Why don't you tell me what question you would LIKE to be asked instead." There was

Blue and white teapot, 20th century. Possibly made in Japan in the style of Qing, with apocryphal or homage seal of Yongzheng. The Yongzheng reign was 1723–1735; the brightness of the colors, however, gives it away as modern-made. Overhead handle, also called stirrup handle or kettle. The motif is "Dragons Sport with Flaming Pearl" or "Dragons Chasing Sacred Pearl" (same thing). Dragons were traditionally used only on wares for the emperor, but by the 16th century had come into common use—provided the dragon had only four claws per foot; five claws were reserved for the emperor. Here you see four.

a short pause while the dealer reclaimed his temper. Then he said, quite calmly and pleasantly, "'What can you tell me about this teapot?'"

And therein lies the decisive point at issue. If you want to become an expert in collecting teapots, if you want to continue the process of learning beyond the acquisition and reading of this book, if you want to be taken seriously as a collector, you will need to learn to navigate the realm of people who know what they're talking about. Because you'll want to know what they know. And the surest way to get them to tell you what they know is to play by their rules.

To test this theory, I went to an antiques emporium in Stamford, Connecticut, with my blue-and-white teapot with the Chinese inscription on the bottom. Instead of introducing myself as I usually do ("Hi-I'm-Leah-Rousmaniere-and-I'm-writing-the-Instant-Expert-volume-on-collecting-teapots-for-Random-House."), I took a more incognito approach. Boldly proffering my teapot, I said, without any introduction whatsoever, "I wonder if you could help me. I'd like to learn more about my teapot—would you have any advice?"

Chinese backstamp on bottom of blue and white teapot. "Made during the Yongzheng reign of the great Qing dynasty." Despite no previous familiarity with the Chinese language, the author was able to decipher the inscription with the aid of Gerald Davidson's *The Handbook of Marks on Chinese Ceramics*.

As luck would have it, the antiques emporium's resident Chinese-export-porcelain expert was present that day, and the saleswoman I approached called her over. She couldn't have been nicer or more helpful. She told me that the teapot was a 20th-century creation despite its "Made during the Yongzheng reign of the great Qing dynasty" mark; that the mark had probably been stamped; that the pot was "definitely porcelain" (I asked because I didn't think it "rang"); and that it may have been made in Japan, which she deducted from the brightness of the pot's colors. She pointed out for comparison a Chinese-export-porcelain plate in a nearby display case, with its more muted blue and slightly-bluish white. When I asked if my teapot was "Canton style," the expert said no, then went on to explain about Cantonware and its particular "look."

I didn't ask the expert what my teapot was worth—although I could have, at the end of the conversation. I'm sure she would have been kind enough to break the bad news gently: very little, because one of the lizards at the base of the handle was missing three of his four feet and half his tail (lost years ago during some skirmish with a Calphalon pot in the dishwasher). Plus, I already knew what I had paid for it—about $35.00—when I bought it new back in the mid-1980s.

I tell you this story to illustrate two points: one, that most dealer-experts are friendly and helpful, so you needn't fear approaching one (even the dealer who yelled at me about price guides gave me a fabulously erudite lesson in pottery and porcelain after he calmed down); and two, that even after speaking with a knowledgeable dealer-expert, you may not have learned everything you want to know about your teapot.

Teapot identification is an art, not a science. Some teapots are more "knowable" than others. While I would love it if someone could tell me something more definitive than "porcelain, late 20th century, China or Japan" about my teapot, I doubt anyone will be able to—there just isn't enough to go on for some teapots. So I'll count myself lucky for my learning experience, and I'll go on enjoying my teapot even if I don't know where or when exactly it was made, or by whom, and even if it is virtually worthless because I was dumb enough to put it in the dishwasher.

The answer to "What's it worth?" is really an amalgam. What are similar teapots listed for in the price guides? What are they selling for in antiques shops? What are they going for on eBay? See "Analyzing the Marketplace: Where and How to Buy and Sell" in Chapter 2 and "Recent Prices" in the back of the book. Ultimately, however, what any given teapot is worth will be up to you. Only you will be able to say whether that "as is" World War II–era "War-Against-Hitlerism" teapot with a broken lid (expertly repaired), considerable tea stains inside, and a small amount of crazing is a steal at $95.00—or an overpriced garage sale has-been, given its flaws. ◙

2

HOW TO THINK AND TALK LIKE AN EXPERT

Remember homework in high school and how tedious it was? That homework was boring only because "they" were making you do it, and the subject wasn't any fun (my personal nemesis: anatomy of the earthworm). When you're interested in the topic, homework can be entertaining and more absorbing than reading a good book, viewing an engaging movie, or surfing the Internet.

While most books and articles on collectibles quote experts telling you to "do your homework," few spell out for you exactly what that homework is or should be.

That's because it depends on what you want to collect.

If you want to collect Chinese-export-porcelain teapots, for example, your homework will consist of:

- learning the history of Chinese export porcelain
- becoming familiar with the types of marks found on Chinese export porcelain
- learning the prevalent patterns (blue and white, Fitzhugh, famille rose)
- visiting museums and antiques shops
- surfing the Internet auctions for current prices

If you want to collect Cardew design teapots, your homework will probably include:

- joining the Cardew Collectors Club and reading their materials
- corresponding with other club members
- visiting various Cardew-related Web sites
- cruising garage sales, second-hand shops, and flea markets "just in case"
- surfing the Internet auctions for current prices

The bottom line: Homework is whatever you need to do to know what's out there; homework is acquiring the vocabulary you need to talk about it; and homework is keeping up with whatever is current.

But before you do any homework, you need to decide what you want to collect.

What to Collect

We all harbor fantasies of discovering some teapot "find" at a garage sale, buying it for $25.00, then taking it on *Antiques Roadshow* only to be told that it's worth thousands. But let's be realistic. Tina M. Carter probably says it best in her book *Collectible Teapots: A Reference and Price Guide*: "If you want a fast return on your investment, teapots may not be the way to go."

While it is true that there has been an upturn in the market value of all things collectible, and that there has been a boom in books on collecting in recent years, and a

American craft teapot, ca. 1920s. Many collectors consider early 20th-century American pottery teapots really hot. While current prices run in the low four figures, someone holding a garage sale might not know that—and may be willing to part with "that old teapot" for a fraction of its true worth. Teapot courtesy of Miriam Novalle, T Salon & T Emporium.

vastly increased interest in antiques and crafts fairs, and that people do collect and have always collected for investment, collecting for investment is a little bit like buying gold for investment: first you have to have the money to buy the gold, then you need to have some place to store it. Can you really afford that $8,500.00, 18th-century Meissen Cockerel teapot? Where will you put it once you get it home? How will you protect your investment? What about insurance? (I don't know about you, but questions like these would keep me awake nights.) If you can afford it and you can take care of it, by all means, buy it. Any 18th-century Meissen teapot is an excellent investment.

Investing on a smaller scale than Meissen is always a possibility, even for people with limited budgets, but you should give up any idea of making a killing until you really know what you're doing. Also, you should anticipate holding any investment item for years before it appreciates, although "years" can be relative. Avant-garde potters like Richard Parrington, Roger Mitchell, and Andy Titcomb produced any number of craft teapots in the 1970s and 1980s, among them the Parrington Princess Diana teapot, which recently sold on eBay for £100.00 without a lid. (£100.00 = $160.52 at conversation rates at this writing.) The Luck and Flaw Margaret Thatcher teapot made by Carlton Ware in the early 1980s has been selling briskly;

recent eBay prices range from $108.00 to $465.00. Are these good investments, however? Not necessarily. They're good investments for the people who already own them and are in a position to sell. But the idea is to buy low, sell high—not buy high and see if the price goes higher. If the price is already high, chances are you've missed the boat; this is true of teapots as well as of stocks.

You may well ask, who in the early 1980s could have predicted that the Luck and Flaw Margaret Thatcher teapot would become such a hit? That's the question, of course. If you could predict market trends like that, you could make money on anything. But you're assuming that the people now selling the Princess Di and Maggie Thatcher teapots bought them as investments. While it's possible some did, I'm willing to bet most didn't. I think it's much more likely they bought them because they admired Princess Di or Lady Thatcher, or they thought the teapots were entertaining, or friends gave them as gag gifts, or who knows whatever other mundane reason.

I know a man who collects first-edition signed mystery novels by previously unpublished authors. Over the years he has seen some volumes appreciate tremendously as their authors went on to become famous. But that's not because he knew who would become famous. It's because he bought indiscriminately. He likes to read; why not? If he counted up how much he has spent over the years on first-edition books by previously unpublished authors, and compared it with how much he might make if he sold the books of the now-famous authors, I doubt he would realize much profit. Does that make him an unsuccessful collector? Hardly.

This collector is successful because he buys what he likes. And really that is the only answer to the question "What should I collect?" What you like. Something you'll take pleasure in having. Something that is worth the hunt, worth the wait, worth the time and effort. Most of all, something that is *you*. As Leslie Ferrin recently told Joyce Lovelace (writing for *American Style Magazine*), "Collectors shape their collections the same way that artists shape their bodies of work. Collecting is their creative output, so [choosing what to collect] can bring a great deal of enjoyment."

Robert Cumming in *Christie's Guide to Collecting* offers these helpful thoughts:

"Collectors need courage, patience, energy, individuality and perhaps a touch of madness. An endless supply of money is fortunately not necessary. Many of the most exciting collections have been built on a modest income. Many of the dullest have been built with a limitless cheque book . . . What matters is the collector with, say, just a few pieces, who has a passion for each one; or the collection that includes among its priceless objects things that are ridiculous, wrong and in bad taste, the despair of uncomprehending friends and advisors, but there because the collector wants them, and because, like the treasures, they have personal meaning; or the collection which has no great amount of objects or financial value, but which is the extension and revelation of an individual's character."

The fabulous thing about collecting, Cumming sums up, "is that virtually anything is worth trying, and nothing is too insignificant or too grand for consideration."

Recent advice published in the *Toronto Star* by Neil Cochrane is worth repeating: "Specialize: put together a unique collection by defining an area before anyone else does." As an example, Cochrane suggests glass teapots and stainless steel tea sets produced in the mid-20th century; these are a good buy at present, and may be a decent investment if you hold onto them long enough. Whether they ever become so popular that they sell for five or six times what you paid for them is a question perhaps best left to the investment gods. Better questions to ask yourself would be: Do I love glass teapots and stainless steel tea sets? Are these items that I want to live with? Do they engage my passions and sentiments? Would a collection of them reflect who I am and the way I see myself?

One caveat on the topic of collecting what you like comes from Vince McDonald of *www.totallyteapots.com*: "If you collect what you like and there are thousands of them made, they never truly become collectible." Best to be a tad more specific than, say, so-called limited editions of 7,500 of the big-name designers' latest offerings. As Robert Rintoul reminds us, "It is a good indication that the large editions of 5,000 or 7,500 do not sell out

Cardew Crime Writer's Desk. Marked on the bottom "05 97, Cardew Designs, Made in England, Limited Edition E1548/3000," and signed by P. Cardew. Robert Rintoul would consider the edition of 3,000 too large to be truly collectible, but this pot was very popular among members of Mystery Writers of America, Sisters in Crime, and other crime writers' organizations.

when the day after you see them on eBay selling at a fraction of the list price. Those same teapots are also frequently found in discount houses like T. J. Maxx at very low prices. For this reason, I stay clear of editions any larger than 2,500."

One major consideration in the What-to-Collect department is your bank account. Dealer Rufus Foshee points out, "Unless one has very substantial money, there is no hope for collecting eighteenth century teapots." Foshee continues, "many people begin with delusion. Their eye may be good and they may like beautiful eighteenth century teapots, but they can't afford them." The solution? When it comes to the 18th century, porcelain currently is cheaper than pottery. If you have a limited budget and you want early pieces, Foshee advises, you'd do much better to buy porcelain.

Luckily, as Lovelace writes, "There's a teapot to suit every taste and pocketbook—commercially produced novelties for a few dollars, handmade wares for hundreds, works by established ceramics artists for thousands, and historical treasures for up to six figures."

One thing you should *not* do is get carried away. It's easy once you confess an enthusiasm for something to rush out and indulge it, torpedoes be damned; if you don't at least have ten or twenty of whatever, after all, how can you take yourself seriously as a collector? Resist that thought. I can tell you that a few years of uninhibited and nondiscriminatory acquisition of Royal Commemoratives put me into something of a pickle; I woke up one morning only to discover that I didn't love some of them. Unfortunately those were precisely the ones then selling for less than I had paid for them. They now reside on the top shelves of kitchen cabinets and behind books in the bookcases while I wonder what to do with them, and kick myself for having bought them in the first place. Keep that in mind when you find yourself lusting after an elephant teapot that has nothing to recommend itself other than that it's an elephant teapot. Think before you buy.

A note about developing an eye: Dealers and experts sometimes wax euphoric about "following your eye," "forming your own judgment," and "having a good look before you decide," entirely forgetting their own salad days, when they didn't know anything either. How can you follow your eye if you don't know what you're looking at, or form your own judgment when you're still clueless? Robert Cumming offers this pointed reminder: "If you take up golf or tennis, you hit the ball the first day whether you know what you're doing or not. Then with practice and instruction, you eventually get better at hitting it. You may even discover you're gifted at hitting it. Or you may not be gifted, but you'll become good enough to play a round or game at the club." Collecting is like that. Only instead of hitting the ball, you're going to be looking at teapots.

The teapot you want to buy may not be the kind sold by antiques stores, but if you want to collect ceramics, you need to get out there and look at ceramics face to face. You can look at pictures in books and on the Internet, but you'll miss the tactile experience doing that, and all the little details that don't show up in printed or digital images. In a shop you can handle the teapot—carefully, and if you turn it upside down, do make sure you hold the lid in place—and see it life-size and three-dimensional. Plus you'll get a real feel for colors and glazes that just don't come across right in photos. Need I add that cruising antiques shops is also more fun than surfing the Internet?

A connoisseur, says Cumming, is "literally 'one who knows.'" He continues:

"There are no shortcuts to developing an eye . . . Two qualities are needed: a willingness to get out and about and look at things firsthand, which is time- and energy-consuming; and the courage to form an incorrect opinion and then discover why it is wrong."

Do not, Cumming cautions, read the label first and then view the object. On the contrary, look at the object and form an opinion, *then* read the label.

In case you haven't already noticed, the teapots that I'm personally interested in are antiques: pre-20th century. I don't so much collect them as visit them in museums, antiques shops, and tea emporia, and as photos in books and posted on Web sites. I'm always cruising for a teapot I can admire and be intrigued by.

You, however, may still be waiting for me to tell you precisely what you *should* buy. You may even be rolling your eyes at advice to collect what you like. There are many, many categories of teapots. Los Angeles businessman Sonny Kamm, who with his wife, Gloria, has put together an astonishing collection of more than 6,000 teapots, and who confesses to buying on average "one or two teapots a day," says he is "on a quest to find a teapot in every material known to man." I suggest you set your sights on a collection somewhat more circumscribed. Flip through this book and see what appeals. Visit antiques shops. Cruise the Internet. Hone your sights. Specialize, be realistic, and pace yourself. Look. Listen. And learn.

Somewhere out there, there's a teapot with your name on it, calling for you.

You'll know it when you see it.

Conservation, Restoration, Care, and Display Guidelines

Generally, *conservation* is what you do to museum pieces to prevent further damage or deterioration; no attempt is made to disguise the repair. *Restoration* not only repairs the item, but paints over the area so you can't see where it's been fixed. Not everyone agrees on terminology. The

Sotheby's Web site calls conservation "museum restoration" and restoration "disguise restoration," elaborating, "museum restoration does not fully conceal damage and is the most desirable to serious collectors." Whether you are a serious collector by Sotheby's standards (collecting teapots that otherwise might find homes in museums), or a collector who loves, displays, lives with, and even uses your teapots, the first thing to learn is how to take care of your pots so they won't need conservation or restoration.

Everyone recommends a display cabinet rather than open shelving, because cabinets help prevent dust. If you don't have a display cabinet, the best way to dust your teapots is with a soft paintbrush or a good shaving brush. Sotheby's recommends that you not pick up your pots by the handle or spout; rather, "lift pieces by their bodies." They also advise removing lids before lifting.

You should not wear gloves when handling ceramics; gloves can be slippery. Your hands should be clean, especially when handling porous earthenware, which can absorb oils. It's a good idea to remove your rings and bracelets before you clean your teapots. Dusting with a brush should be enough. If you need to wash your teapot, however, you should use warm water, not hot. Hot water can damage repairs, especially if the repairs are old. Use gentle detergent, which means dish soap. Sotheby's advises that you never wash unglazed porous earthenware, just wipe it with a damp cloth.

If all this seems a bit la-dee-da, remember that Sotheby's deals with and cares for expensive antiques. Your teapots may be neither expensive nor antique, and they may even be dishwasher safe—in which case, go right ahead and put them in the dishwasher. Just be sure to prevent them from knocking against other items. (A supply of Tupperware lids is good for this purpose.) The operating principle is always to use good common sense.

Gaynor Laight of www.crackedchina.co.uk advises washing your teapots in a plastic basin lined with a foam mat rather than in the sink, where the teapot could crash against the faucets, or you could drop it on the hard bottom. Laight uses an old toothbrush to scrub awkward places. "Really fragile pieces should be cleaned by wiping them gently with cotton wool," Laight says. "If it's stained, try a solution of hydrogen peroxide, but take great care. If a piece is gilded, be really careful, this can come off—so do not use cleaning agents." Laight once bleached the inside of an old teapot to get rid of tea stains; "I now know better," she rues. "If you're going to use hydrogen peroxide, wear gloves."

Sotheby's says no gloves—but somehow I don't think they're cleaning anything with peroxide. You're going to have to evaluate the advice you get and make your own decisions based on your personal risk-factor quotient and your individual teapot. Jerry McCracken in an article posted on *www.antiqueresources.com* blithely advises submerging your tired-looking pottery in a bucket filled with Peroxide #40, available at your local beauty supply store. "If your pottery is very dirty," he says, "it may take days or even weeks to become clean. Don't worry about your item. The peroxide won't harm [it]." One can only imagine the entire team of Sotheby's experts lined up like so many Edvard Munch paintings of *The Scream* at such a prospect. Yet McCracken, proprietor of Artisan Antiques, must know what he's talking about.

McCracken agrees with Laight: "NEVER use BLEACH!" Andrea Daley in an article also posted on *www. AntiqueResources.com*, however, has no compunction about using "bleach spray cleaner" on unglazed or bisque porcelain, although she does advise "Never use a bleach spray cleaner first. Use only after an all purpose cleaner. If bleach cleaner is used first it may set a stain." Daley is the owner of Restorers of America Inc., "with over 31 dedicated years of service in the field." I assume she knows what she's talking about, too. Again, your choice.

Personally, I wash everything with dish soap and water, and let it soak for five to ten minutes first. My oldest pieces are late Victorian (around 1900). Everything gets washed three times a year: once before Passover, once before Rosh Hashanah, and once before Christmas. (Mixed marriage; we do all the holidays.) In between, I dust with a soft paintbrush.

Once your teapots are dusted or washed and dried (drip-drying on a rack is recommended if you're going to wash them, although I confess I carefully dry mine with cotton tea towels), you will want to put them back in their display cabinet or on their shelf. It goes without saying not to display your teapots on the radiator cabinet, or on a windowsill where they get direct sunlight. Extremes of heat and cold are a big no-no; for this reason, you should avoid storing teapots either in the garage or in the attic. Temperature extremes can cause crazing and cracking, as can direct sunlight. If you do have to store your teapots for whatever reason, DO NOT wrap them in newspaper. Newspaper can stain ceramics and turn some glazes coffee-colored. Use bubble wrap or acid-free tissue or paper instead.

If your teapot has historic value and you break it, take it to a professional. If you acquire a historic teapot that has been restored, it's probably a good idea not to wash it. Old glues may be especially fragile. Depending on the value of your teapot, you may or may not want to try fixing it yourself.

Gaynor Laight recommends taking a course in conservation and restoration; she herself studied with a china restorer and now makes her own museum repairs. Laight confides, "I have not attempted to paint them, but I am hoping to undertake further training and perhaps paint those pieces that need painting!" Sounds good to me, and I'm going to put "Conservation Class" on my own to-do list.

The American Institute for Conservation of Historic and Artistic Works can assist you in finding a conservator or restorer near you if you need one. Visit their Web site, *www.aic-faic.org,* and click on "Selecting a Conservator." Or call them at 202-452-9545. You may also E-mail them with questions at info@aic-faic.org.

Essential Vocabulary

If you're going to converse with experts and dealers about teapots, you should make an effort to sound like you know what you're talking about. The best way to sound like you know what you're talking about is to actually *know* what you're talking about.

King's Arms Tavern teapot. Modern reproduction by Williamsburg of a teapot shape popular both in England and the Colonies in the late 17th century. Arms are those of the British royal family, with mottos "Honi Soit Que Mal Y Pense" and "Dieu et Mon Droit," undoubtedly applied by transfer. A teabag teapot without strainer at base of spout.

Luckily with teapots there isn't a lot of lingo to learn. You already know the basics: *spout, body, handle, lid.* The under-rim of the lid is sometimes called the *inside flange of the teapot lid,* and where you pour the water in is the *filling aperture.* The knob on the lid is the *finial.* The end of the handle where it connects with the body is sometimes called the *terminal,* especially with handles where the terminal is a decorative flourish like a bunch of leaves or flowers.

If you want to collect historic teapots, say, Chinese export, Minton Majolica, or 18th-century Wedgwood, you will want to familiarize yourself with language used by dealers, museum curators, and decorative-arts experts. For example, blue and white Chinese export porcelain is generally called *underglaze blue, hard paste* by museums. There are technical words for various shapes and handles, such as *conical spout, globular,* and *overhead handle,* which you can study by reading captions in this book, looking in the Index under "Shape," perusing descriptions of teapots on Web sites, and reading labels in museums and antiques shops.

Now may be a good time to pass on advice first proffered by New York dealer Paul Vandekar and Lisa Hubbard in a recently published article in *Martha Stewart Living*: "Put off mastering the terminology and concentrate instead on studying export pieces in person. 'Don't be narrow about what you want to collect; develop your own taste,' Vandekar says. Once you understand what interests you, it's easy to learn the words to describe it." This advice rings true for any sub-genre of teapot, from racing-car teapots, to cottage teapots, to novelty teapots that don't actually pour, and to the Luck and Flaw Ronald Reagan and Margaret Thatcher teapots.

I do urge you to learn a few ceramics terms. See "Pottery or Porcelain?" and "What Condition Is It In?" in Chapter 1. Also in Chapter 1, "Does It Say Anything on the Bottom?" explains terms you'll need to know about marks. As you make your way through this book, you will find that terminology—even that used by museum curators, antiques dealers, and decorative-arts experts—can be haphazard, confusing, and contradictory. Read the section on whatever kind of teapot interests you; any terms I think you should know will be discussed there. Definitions are repeated in the Glossary.

Analyzing the Marketplace: Where and How to Buy and Sell

Before you buy or sell a teapot, you'll want to know what the going prices are for teapots like it. Robert Rintoul, in an article posted at *www.totallyteapots2.com*, advises watching the eBay auctions. He monitors not only the sales of teapots he'd like to buy, but also those of teapots he already owns. "With teapots I already have in my collection, when the auction ends, I print out the listing with the closing price and place it in a special file that allows me to keep tabs on current prices of teapots I own," Rintoul writes. "As to the unusual teapots that I do not wish to purchase, those go into a separate file as reference material. Then, for example, if I didn't buy the first time around due to a shortage of funds, if one appears again for sale at a later date and I am then in a position to buy, I have an idea of what I will have to spend."

Watching the eBay auctions also gives Rintoul a "pretty good idea of what is a rare item" and, after the auction, what it should sell for. This knowledge allows him to pick up teapots at antiques shows where dealers who don't watch the eBay auctions may be selling the same thing for less than it would sell for on eBay.

Which brings me to another point: Any given teapot can fetch a range of prices, depending on where you buy or sell it. An antiques shop in a high-rent big city (Boston, say, or New York) is probably going to charge more for virtually the same teapot than a "grandmother's-attic" shop on a rambling country road in Ohio. But if you're standing in an antiques shop in Boston holding the teapot of your dreams in your hands, wouldn't it be cheaper to pay the premium price in Boston than to get in your car, drive to Ohio, and cruise the grandmother's-attic shops there in hopes of finding its twin brother or sister? If you haven't done your homework, and don't already know the price range for the teapot of your dreams, you can always ask the antiques shop to hold the item for 12 hours while you consult your husband, wife, or partner about buying it. If, however, after a mad dash to the nearest public library to check out prices on the Internet, you decide not to buy the teapot, make sure you call the shop to thank it for holding it for you and to convey your regrets.

The Kovels' price guides are always worth consulting, and *www.kovels.com* offers a free newsletter and free registration to download prices cited on the Web site. As Tina M. Carter reminds us in her valuable reference and price guide *Collectible Teapots*, however, "The value of any given object is what the buyer is willing to pay." A price guide is just that: a guide.

See "Recent Prices" in the back of this book for some recent teapot prices.

Fakes, Forgeries, and Reproductions

David Battie, in *David Battie's Guide to Understanding 19th and 20th Century British Porcelain: Including Fakes, Techniques, and Prices*, draws a distinction between fakes and forgeries: "A Fake is a genuine object that has been altered in some way, such as adding decoration or a mark. A Forgery is a fresh, deliberate attempt to deceive." While we're at it, we should also take a moment to consider modern reproductions. Sometimes used as a euphemism for forgeries, *modern reproduction* as a class also broadly includes items like the Minton

Minton Majolica Vulture & Python teapot. Sometimes also called Bird of Prey with Snake, ca. 1880. Photo Courtesy Rufus Foshee.

Archives Vulture & Python teapot. A late-20th-century copy of the 19th-century original, it is marked as such on the base (the key word is *Archives*) and is sold by the now-owner of Minton, Royal Doulton, without pretense. Many collectors, unable to cough up the £46,875.00 ($75,242.50 at conversion rates at this writing) that an original Vulture & Python teapot sold for recently at Christie's, might be perfectly happy to shell out £495.00 ($794.56) for an Archives edition copy. And why not?

Unfortunately, there are unscrupulous sellers of teapots out there who, unlike Royal Doulton, do not tell prospective buyers up front that a given teapot is in fact a modern reproduction and not the hoped-for antique or collector's item. Some of these unscrupulous sellers are, alas, reputable art dealers. Some have fooled some extremely sophisticated collectors, including Mr. and Mrs. Henry Weldon, who have one of the finest collections of English pottery in private hands.

According to Lita Solis-Cohen in her article for *Maine Antique Digest*, "Designed to Deceive," when the authenticity of one of the Weldons' coffeepots was called into question at a 1991 Ceramics Fair in London, the Weldons submitted the pot to thermoluminescence tests, only to find out that the pot in question was less than 100 years old. During the investigation that followed, further testing turned up 40 more forgeries acquired by prominent (read: sophisticated and wealthy) collectors. Eventually the authorities arrested Guy Timothy Davies, an amateur potter and antiques dealer. "The jury reportedly did not understand the scientific thermoluminescence tests performed at Oxford," Solis-Cohen notes ruefully, "and felt sorry for the poor potter who duped the rich dealers and collectors." Davies was acquitted. Which means he's still out there.

One can thank the Weldons for their community-mindedness; their unwitting purchases of forgeries later became the nexus of an exhibit at the DeWitt Wallace Decorative Arts Gallery at Colonial Williamsburg in Virginia, "Designed to Deceive: English Pottery Fakes!" (David Battie would call them forgeries, not fakes; but as my mother is fond of saying, To Each His or Her Own.) The exhibit, which sets fakes, forgeries, and reproductions side by side with their originals, has unfortunately closed. But Leslie B. Grigsby wrote an excellent large-format book about the Weldons' collection, *English Pottery: Stoneware and Earthenware: 1650–1800*, published by Sotheby's. The book is a must-read for anyone hoping to come up to speed on fakes and forgeries of late-17th- and early-18th-century English teapots, and not a bad item to add to the old to-read list for anyone else.

At this writing, a Seattle gallery, Thesaurus Fine Arts, is under investigation by both the Washington state attorney general and the Federal Trade Commission for selling forgeries, according to Duff Wilson and Sheila Farr of the *Seattle Times*. A doctor, a professor, an archaeologist, and a business leader are among the many Thesaurus buyers who apparently got taken. While investigating, the reporters bought a "Tang dynasty" teapot. That alone should ring alarm bells in any serious teapot collector's head. The first teapots came into being during the Ming dynasty—a good five hundred years after the Tang dynasty ended. Thesaurus Fine Arts unfortunately is not the only dealer under investigation. While most dealers are trustworthy, some are not.

I tell you these tales of woe to warn you against ever believing that you are totally on top of the fakes and forgeries question. Real experts have been fooled. People have lost thousands of dollars buying forgeries. David Battie has this advice: "Each object is best approached with the words: 'You are a forgery, prove to me you are right.'" In other words, forgery until proven otherwise. That said, it is possible to come moderately up to speed vis-à-vis fakes and forgeries. But it takes time and work.

Marks are always a good place to start. Whatever kind of teapot you collect, you should memorize the range of authentic marks and what dates of manufacture are associated with them. Belleek, for example, has a complicated system of marks including "the first version of the eighth mark," which, according to Brian J. Graham of the Belleek Collector's International Society, unfortunately looks "VERY similar to a 2nd black mark." To follow the talk on "Fake Belleek on the Internet," which Graham gave at the September 1999 BCIS convention, you would have to know the difference between these marks—and be able to recognize them when you saw them. Luckily, there are plenty of sources to consult: books on marks, Web sites, other collectors. Not everyone does his or her homework, or knows what he or she is talking about. But if you keep a notebook and write down not only what you learn, but from whom you learn it, pretty soon you'll be able to sort out whom you can trust.

One problem with sellers on Web sites like eBay is that they themselves may not know the difference between the first version of the eighth mark and the second mark—and thus may think they're selling an older object than is indeed the case. As Graham pointed out in his talk, "This leads to incorrect descriptions and can catch the collector who is new to Belleek collecting and has not yet studied the marks closely." Luckily, eBay is extremely diligent when it comes to policing accuracy on its site. In one example cited by Graham, knowledgeable Belleek collectors informed one eBay seller of his/her mistake, and a note was added to the auction advising bidders. The site encourages registered members to report any suspected abuses to its Safe Harbor team of investigators (*www.pages.ebay.com/help/community/investigates.html*). This group reviews the evidence and adjudicates whether there is enough to warrant a suspension or termination from eBay.

"Known examples" are another important resource for any rightly suspicious potential teapot buyer. These are teapots whose authenticity is substantiated by the origi-

Racing car teapot. Modern reproduction made by Racing Teapots Ltd from original mold for Sadler OKT42 car of 1930s. Available at this writing for $98.00 at *www.abitofbritain.com.*

nal manufacturer's specs, or has been verified by experts. Compare the teapot you want to buy with the known example, if only in your head. Pay particular attention to color, size, and style.

The original OKT42 racing car teapot, pre-1947, for example, according to *www.racingteapots.com,* was usually glazed in one color with chrome/platinum painted on the wings, steering wheel and spokes, driver's helmet, and goggles. The car should measure 9.5 inches long, 4.5 inches wide, and 4.5 inches tall. Any teapot not meeting those specifications is a later issue or a forgery or modern reproduction.

The D&RG Curecanti pattern teapot has been faked in a blue version, according to *railroadcollectors.org;* the savvy collector will know that the original teapot was issued in black and brown markings on a white base, had a manufacturer's mark on the bottom, and last dates from the 1920s.

David Battie's Guide to Understanding 19th and 20th Century British Porcelain has a photo of a porcelain figure with the caption "Department of Wishful Thinking." On the bottom of the figure is a mark reading "Flight & Barr" with a crown. "The mark has been painted on in ink and the base given a thick layer of lacquer," the author notes. Pointing out that "no such figure or mark exists and such a deception would be unlikely to fool anyone," he recommends "resorting to a pin or tooth tap," which "will immediately disclose the soft layer of paint or lacquer." While I might not be willing to test items with my teeth in, say, Bergdorf Goodman's seventh-floor Vintage Tea Shop, I suppose it's a technique to keep in mind for garage sales. The pin poke might be a bit more discreet.

It is true that cheap knock-off teapots may be painted on top of the glaze, and that this paint chips off easily. Such a teapot certainly would present fair game for pin-poking by the Teapot Fraud Squad, probably even with satisfactory results (you can almost hear them crowing "ah-HA!" in true Sherlockian fashion). I personally would pass by any such teapot without poking.

Brian Graham warns Belleek collectors to be wary of forged marks applied by transfer. "One dealer found out the hard way that the mark had been added; it came OFF when the piece of Belleek was left soaking in dishwater!" He notes that marks can be altered, as well. "If you see scratch marks on the piece close to the mark, it is possible it has been 'enhanced,'" he warns. "This usually occurs when a 3rd black mark is altered to appear to be a 2nd black mark." With some humor he also notes the would-be forger who misspelled *Belleek*. I suppose it goes without saying that you know how to spell the name of the manufacturer of whatever kind of teapot you collect.

Tina Carter has some good final advice on the topic of fakes and forgeries: "If you're not sure the teapot is authentic, don't buy it until you're able to do some research or unless the price is low enough—under $30.00."

On the other hand you may know it's a forgery and like it anyway. Ian McLachlan, interviewed by Wilson and Farr of the *Seattle Times* for their article exposing the Thesaurus Fine Arts Gallery, told them he knew full well he was buying a fake Chinese bowl. "A real one would be a couple of million, not $250.00. It's a good fake and it gives me a lot of pleasure." McLachlan decided later not to deal with the gallery anymore. "I couldn't get [Thesaurus Fine Arts Gallery] to admit it was a fake," he explained. ◼

3

THE HISTORY OF TEAPOTS AND TEA

The origin of tea is shrouded in myth, legend, and half-truths. One myth tells us that the Chinese Emperor Shen Nung (pronounced shay-nung), on a quest to taste and catalog all the herbs in his kingdom, made himself quite ill—but felt much better after drinking his first cup of tea, brewed accidentally when a few leaves fell off a nearby tea bush into his pot of boiling water. The date was 2737 B.C.E. Perhaps it is remembered so precisely because up until that time, Shen Nung's people, on his orders, had been drinking plain boiled water, which they said tasted like flatirons, in which case the taste of tea would have been a welcome improvement. Tea or no tea, however,

Shen Nung, who had the head of an ox and the body of a man, went on tasting and cataloging herbs with such single-mindedness that he finally died from eating a poisonous one. (There's a moral here somewhere—perhaps that even tea can't cure oxheadedness?)

Another myth tells the story of Bodhidharma, also known as Daruma, a pious prince who lived in India. Sometime around 500 C.E. he set himself the task of contemplating Buddha for nine years, but this proved a more daunting enterprise than he had anticipated, and he kept falling asleep. So he tore off his eyelids and threw them on the ground, whereupon two tea bushes sprang up on the spot. Bodhidharma made himself a cup of tea, and so much for the sleep problem. You do kind of wonder about his eye problem, unless he made himself some new lids out of tea leaves.

Tea was certainly known and consumed in China by the third century C.E., although not in the form that we know it today. For one thing, people didn't drink it then—they ate it. The tea leaves were roasted to a reddish-brown color, pounded in a mortar, and made into a cake, which was then boiled together with salt, rice, ginger, orange peel, spices, and sometimes onions, the end result being a kind of tea-and-rice soup.

By the middle of the Tang dynasty (618–906 C.E.), tea had evolved from a soup to a drink, at least in more sophisticated circles. The method of making teacakes seems to have undergone a refinement process as well; contemporary sources detail an extremely complicated series of steps for steaming or roasting the freshly picked tea leaves: pounding, grinding, or pulverizing them into powder; forming the paste into cakes, bricks, or tablets; and finally, pan-drying the whole. Before being used, the cakes, bricks, or tablets would then have to be reheated by the fire (another process of many steps) and pounded back into powder form. The powder was boiled in water, or put into a cup and boiling water poured over it.

Perhaps because the entire process had become so labyrinthine, tea merchants in the eighth century C.E. commissioned a book on tea. This was the *Cha Ching* (also spelled *Chajing* or *Chaking*), usually called in English "The Classic of Tea" or "Holy Scriptures of Tea." Written by Yu Lu (sometimes spelled Luwuh), the book, in which the origin of tea, the manufacturing process, and the utensils used in making and drinking tea were studied in great detail, is now part of the canon of Chinese literature and learning.

According to the *Cha Ching*, the best quality tea must have creases like the leathern boot of Tartar horsemen, curl like the dewlap of a mighty bullock, unfold like a mist rising out of a ravine, gleam like a lake touched by a zephyr, and be wet and soft like fine earth newly swept by rain.

Tibetan tea brick. Ornate cakes of compressed black tea have been used for centuries as a way to store tea, as a form of currency, and as highly prized gifts. Available at Simpson & Vail. Photo courtesy of Simpson & Vail, Inc., Brookfield, CT 06804, 1-800-282-TEAS.

Yu Lu preferred his tea without any extraneous ingredients, disdaining the rice-tea-onion concoction as "slop-water of a ditch." That didn't bother nomads and travelers on caravan along the famous Silk Road, however. The flat, hard tea bricks were easily transportable and, serrated into squares like a modern-day Hershey bar, could be used as currency in an age before international banks and exchange rates. Sour yak milk and butter came to be included in the soup recipe; a Captain Turner drank that version in Tibet in the 18th century, and various Mongolian tribes still consume it today.

It was during the Sung dynasty (960–1279 C.E.) that the drinking of tea evolved into an art form. As Lo Kuei-hsiang describes it *The Stonewares of Yixing*, "during the Song [Sung] dynasty, the leaves were first ground into a very fine powder . . . after adding boiling water, [the person making the tea] stirred the powder vigorously with a bamboo brush and finally served the tea." This method of preparation, called *whipped* or *whisked* tea, was a refinement on the Tang method of *boiled* tea, but neither method required a teapot. Boiled tea was prepared in a cooking pot, and whipped tea was made in a bowl. Neither was brewed nor steeped. The English words *brew* and *steep* are used to translate Tang and Sung dynasty Chinese manuscripts, but these are loose, rather than technical translations. Powdered tea did not brew or steep; technically, brewing or steeping involves the unfurling of the whole tea leaf.

While boiled tea had been a food and then a drink, during the Sung dynasty whipped tea became a ritual. Buddhist monks began the practice of gathering before the image of Bodhidharma and solemnly drinking tea out of a single bowl; it was this Zen sacrament that eventually developed into the tea ceremony of Japan in the 15th century. Unfortunately, as Okakura Kakuzo recounts in *The Book of Tea*, the Mongol tribes swept into China in the 13th century and "destroyed all the fruits of Sung culture." The Mongols, who founded the Yuan dynasty (1280–1368 C.E.), apparently had no interest in tea; it was during their reign that Marco Polo visited the Imperial Court, but was never served any. Or so scholars believe, based on the premise that had Polo been served tea, he would have written about it in the same lavish detail with which he wrote about everything else. But he doesn't even mention it.

In any case, by the time of the Ming dynasty (1368–1644 C.E.) and the restoration of tea to favor at the Imperial Court, there was a wailing and beating of breasts because the shape of the tea whisk mentioned in the Sung classics had been lost to history. Throughout the Yuan dynasty the Chinese people had continued drinking tea, whisk or no whisk. But somewhere along the way, most tea drinkers seem to have dispensed with cakes, bricks, and tablets. In his book *Caomuzi* (published in 1378 C.E.), Ye Ziqi reported that "people no longer use powdered tea from Jiangxi Province; tea in loose leaf form is preferred everywhere."

Herein sounds the drumroll for teapots. Leaf tea, as opposed to powdered tea, was *rolled*, requiring that it be *brewed* or *steeped* because the flavor releases only as the leaves unfurl in the boiling water. For that, tea drinkers needed a suitable vessel.

You could, of course, brew tea in a bowl, and many people did. A great deal has been written about the change in Chinese ceramics, due apparently to the change in the processing and preparation of tea: the Sung liked blue-black and dark brown bowls, which they felt enhanced the depth of whipped tea; the Ming preferred white porcelain bowls, which better showed the light-colored brewed tea. At the same time, there was a slow evolution in thought toward the teapot.

The Very First Teapot

No one knows when people first started brewing tea in teapots. The teapot prototype was the ewer, a tall, water pitcher–shaped vessel with a lid, not unlike many modern coffeepots. Some scholars, in fact, believe that the teapot prototype was really an Arabian coffeepot that made its way east on the Silk Road. Since the ewer and Arabian coffeepot are pretty much the same shape, we'll never know either way. Both would be suitable for brewing tea; all that would need to happen would be for the proverbial light bulb to go on over someone's head—Hey, we could brew tea in a ewer or a coffeepot instead of in a bowl! After that, it would be only a matter of time before someone realized that round, squat ewers would give the tea leaves more room to unfurl than taller, more oblong ewers, and would thus be better for brewing.

Excavation of a dragon kiln at Yangjiashan in China has recently unearthed a number of unglazed stoneware shards from the Sung dynasty, most fragments of ewers and jars that archaeologists have reassembled into their original forms. Among these reconstituted ewers is one that has a globular body with a dragon spout, a double-band handle, and a flat cover with a button knob—very teapot-like. Another has a round, squat body and overhead handle. A third ewer is hexagonal in shape. All these exemplify the earliest of the basic shapes the first Ming teapots would later take.

There is a story told by a Ming authority, Zhou Gaoqi, that credits the creation of the very first teapot to a monk of the Jinsha temple at Nanshan near Yixing, during the reign of the Ming emperor Zhengde (1505–1521 C.E.). The story is problematic for any number of reasons I won't go into here (if you'd like more information, read further in Lo Kuei-hsiang's book *The Stonewares of Yixing*), but it is true

Yixing teapot of dome shape with six-lobed body. Signature: "Gongchun, dated 8th year of Zhengde period" (1513). Flagstaff House Museum of Tea Ware, Hong Kong Museum of Art Collection. Photo supplied by the Hong Kong Museum of Art.

that monks had long been associated with tea. And the scholar class, who would shortly become the first teapot enthusiasts, had a longstanding acquaintance with monks. So it stands to reason that a monk made the first teapot.

The earliest example of a teapot that has survived to this day seems to be the one in the Flagstaff House Museum of Tea Ware (Hong Kong Museum of Art). The pot is attributed to Gongchun and dated 1513—the middle Ming period. Gongchun is considered the father of the *zisha* teapot, what we would call a Yixing (pronounced ee-shing or yee-shing) teapot; *zisha* is the type of clay used to make Yixing pottery. Tradition has it that Gongchun was a boy-servant to the scholar Wu Yishan, who studied at the Jinsha temple. While his master was busy, the boy spent his free time watching the monk potters working at their kiln. Gongchun learned to make teapots; his master went on to become a scholar and high administrative official. The master had many literary and artistic friends, and the teapots came to the attention of the literati and glitterati. Gongchun became possibly the most famous tea-potter of all time.

I would like to take a moment now to debunk the idea, astonishingly prevalent among even some of the most highly respected authorities on pottery and porcelain, that the Chinese were still brewing tea in bowls when some Western European got the idea to order from Macao, Amoy, or Batavia a ewer-type vessel with a tea strainer at the base of the spout, thus "inventing" the first teapot. This is nonsense. While it is true that early

Chinese teapots did not have strainers at the base of the spout, and that European ladies did not like picking pieces of tea leaf out of their teeth, and that the idea to make teapots with strainers at the base of the spout *may* have originated with one of these ladies' husbands—or possibly with one of the ladies themselves—the Chinese invented the teapot. Tea did not come to Western Europe until nearly a century after Gongchun made the teapot now in the Hong Kong Museum. When the Chinese sent their first shipments of tea to Europe, they thoughtfully included both *zisha* and porcelain teapots. The first teapots made in Europe were modeled on the Chinese teapots. Case closed.

Yixing Teapots

When we think of Asian teapots, we often think of Chinese porcelain pots, lovely and delicate, usually blue and white, or perhaps painted with traditional Chinese scenes in exquisite, muted colors. But the original teapot was the *zisha* or Yixing teapot, humbly made by monks, unglazed and undecorated, treasured by scholars who knew how to appreciate the simple things in life.

Yixing is a small town in the Chinese province of Jiangsu, halfway between Shanghai and Nanjing (a.k.a. Nanking or Nankeen), near the west bank of Lake Taihu. The town gave its name to both the surrounding region and the pottery produced there, and is variously spelled in English Yixing, Xising, Yihsing, I-hsing, Yi-hsing—and possibly a few other ways I haven't run across yet. (These various spellings are something to keep in mind when doing Internet searches.) The Jiangsu province is the world's only source for the unique *zisha* clay, also called purple or red clay. *Zisha* clay actually comprises a range of colors from *banshanlu* (buff-colored) to *zhusha* (cinnabar or deep orange-red) to *zisha* purple, but the most highly prized is the purple. The pottery made from *zisha* can be called Yixing, redware, or red stoneware; 17th-century Europeans called it *boccarro* or "redd porcelain." It's all basically the same stuff.

Zisha clay's unique properties make it ideal for brewing tea. Fired unglazed, it's very porous, so any teapot made from it will absorb the color, smell, and flavor of the tea brewed in it. For this reason, tea enthusiasts often have a small collection of Yixing teapots, one solely for each flavor of tea they drink. The teapots become seasoned after repeated use, adding to the taste of the brew. They are never washed with soap or any other kind of cleanser, only rinsed with water and inverted to drain. Truly dedicated Yixing teapot owners use only water free of undesirable contaminants (e.g., chlorine), both for brewing and rinsing.

By Western standards Yixing teapots are relatively small. Simon K.S. Chiu, in his essay "Tea Drinking in China" (*The Art of the Yixing Potter: The K.S. Lo Collection, Flagstaff House Museum of Tea Ware*, Hong Kong Museum of Art), explains why: "In the beginning these teapots were relatively large, but their size soon proved to be a disadvantage, for by the time one got to the bottom of the pot, the leaves had been steeped for too long and the tea had lost its freshness or had even turned acrid. Teapots became smaller in size." I suggest another possible reason Yixing teapots are small: the very first teapot owners were monks and scholars. In my mind I see them hunched over their sacred texts, scribbling notes and writing treatises, burning the midnight oil—alone with their individual serving–sized pots of tea. Research and writing have always been solitary activities.

Today's Yixing teapots still brew an individual serving, as opposed to European-style teapots that are often large enough to serve an entire tea party of a half-dozen people.

In the latter part of the 19th century, the Yixing potteries suffered from increasing industrialization and fell into decline. Potters were instructed by unscrupulous bosses to produce teapots that could be "attributed" to the old masters—and sold as if they were the real thing. Other potters went on turning out the time-worn old designs; there was very little creative new design. The potteries were closed entirely by invading Japanese forces during World War II. But luckily for tea and teapot lovers everywhere, the Yixing pottery industry was reopened and revitalized by the People's Republic of China in the 1950s. There was an outburst of new creativity, new enthusiasm, and new inspiration, and many new teapot designs were added to the Yixing potter's repertoire. At the same time, the designs that had been considered time-worn

Yixing Bamboo Tablet teapot, 21st century. Strainer at base of spout, artist's chop mark on bottom, also paper label "Made in China." Available at this writing for $76.00 at T Salon and T Emporium, 1-888-NYCTEAS.

returned to their former rightful place as classics.

Nowadays, Yixing *zisha* teapots are made the way they have always been made: formed by hand, from a single sheet of clay, the bottom of the teapot stamped with the potter's own mark or chop. Both new and old designs are available from the many shops and Web sites selling Yixing teapots. A few years ago, Zhou Jiazhou (quoted by Lo Kuei-hsiang) had this to say about modern Yixing teapot production:

"Yixing teapots have many shapes. They can be round, square, angular, flat, level, lofty, low, big or small, egg-like . . . On examination of their quality, some will be found to be warm and genial like old gentlemen, some brave as heroes, some stylish as men of letters, beautiful as pretty girls, lovely as children, small as pygmies, simple and slow like old men, jaunty and fanciful as fairies, austere as philosophers, others are unworldly like Buddhist priests, [but] connoisseurs and collectors must love them in their hearts before one can discuss with them such delights."

Porcelain Teapots, Tea, and the First English Teapot

While Yixing *zisha* teapots may have been first on the teapot map, they soon had competition from teapots made of porcelain, and from ewers and wine pots that could just as easily be used to brew tea. We know that the tiny *zisha* teapots were used exclusively to brew tea;

porcelain teapots, however, are harder to conclusively identify. A telltale indicator that a pot was made to brew tea is a strainer at the base of the spout. But if strainers were an innovation demanded by European taste, and not common until the early to mid-18th century, we come face to face with a conundrum: is a 16th- or 17th-century Chinese porcelain pot a teapot if it doesn't have a strainer at the base of the spout?

Many conservative experts would say no.

What about Chinese porcelain pots made *before* strainers came into vogue?

Well, those would be ewers or wine pots.

I found this reasoning maddeningly Eurocentric (of the same ilk as "Europeans-invented-the-teapot"), until I visited the Web site of the Flagstaff Museum of Tea Ware in Hong Kong, where I was able to view several very teapot-like ewers and wine pots. Bottom line: If an antique porcelain pot doesn't have a strainer, conservative experts won't *definitively* classify it as a teapot. We know that Chinese people in the 16th and 17th centuries often brewed tea in their porcelain ewers and wine pots—and may even have considered them TEApots—but we don't know it in terms of scholarly certainty, or on an individual basis for each and every ewer or wine pot. Keep this in mind when you visit museums to view early examples of Chinese export porcelain.

Porcelain predates teapots by centuries; the first porcelain was probably made during the Sui (581–617 C.E.) or early Tang (618–906 C.E.) dynasties. The word itself—*porcelain*—made its way into the English language first via the Italian (*porcellana*), then the French (*porcelaine*), and originated with Marco Polo, who visited China at the outset of the Yuan dynasty in the late 13th century and had this to say:

"Let me tell you further that in this province, in a city called Tinju, they make bowls of *porcellana*, large and small, of incomparable beauty . . . These dishes are made of a crumbly earth or clay which is dug as though from a mine and stacked in huge mounds and then left for thirty or forty years exposed to wind, rain and sun. By this time the earth is so refined that dishes made of it are of an azure tint with a very brilliant sheen. You must understand that when a man makes a mound of this earth he does so for his children."

Porcellana was a word eminently understandable by Marco Polo's readers: in Italian it meant "little pig" and was the name of a pink seashell that inside was translucent and shiny, much like the Chinese bowls Polo was describing. (In English these shells are called cowrie shells, and they are so universally known that I had a bracelet made of them when I was a kid.)

Over the course of the 17th century, both tea and porcelain began to make their way to Western Europe, and from there to the Dutch colony of New Amsterdam in the Americas. For some reason the English were not at first taken by tea; at least, the directors of the English East India Company saw no reason to import it (they were more interested in pepper), even though the Dutch East India Company was doing a brisk business in both Chinese and Japanese tea in the Netherlands by the mid-1630s, when tea was also all the rave in Paris. Small amounts of tea did make their way into England either from Holland or as officially permitted private trade—the private investments of a ship's officers and crew. Employees of the East India Company returning from India and China undoubtedly brought tea with them as well. In any case, enough tea arrived on English shores to come to the attention to the coffeehouse keepers whose establishments sprung up in and around London's Exchange Alley after 1650. (I have already mentioned the Sultaness-Head, first to advertise tea in 1658.)

Tea as served in coffeehouses was brewed in large quantities and stored in kegs like beer. The first taxes on tea were levied by the government to replace lost revenues from beer and ale, which were taxed by the gallon, so tea likewise was taxed by the gallon. Before tea, people in England from royalty on down drank beer and ale for breakfast and for every meal thereafter (unless they could afford wine) because water supplies were contaminated. We can only imagine their awe when they discovered that tea not only didn't pickle you, but actually woke you up! Moreover, in an age when disease and sanitation were poorly understood, tea was made from boiled water, which was actually safe to drink.

Little wonder then, that tea became the health drink *ne plus ultra* and panacea for any number of ills. Thomas Garway's famous "An Exact Description of the Growth, Quality and Vertues of the Leaf TEA," published as a broadside in 1660, sang the praises of tea to the proverbial high heavens:

"It maketh the body active and lusty. It helpeth the Headache, giddiness and heavyness thereof. It removeth the obstructions of the Spleen. It is very good against the Stone and Gravel, cleaning the Kidneys and Uriters . . . It taketh away the difficulty of breathing, opening Obstructions . . ."

And on and on, concluding effusively:

"that the Vertues and excellencies of this Leaf and Drink are many and great is evident and manifest by the high esteem and use of it (especially of late years) among the Physitians and knowing men in France, Italy, Holland and other parts of Christendom."

One extremely interesting item to note: Tea, according to Garway, "being prepared with milk and water strengtheneth the inward parts." This statement establishes that tea was drunk with milk in England as early as 1660—twenty years earlier than Madam de Sévigné's 1680 letter crediting Madame de la Salabière with the idea of mixing milk with her tea, often considered the earliest record of the use of milk in tea in Europe. Purists may argue that tea taken for medicinal purposes and tea drunk as a beverage are two separate entities; they may credit Madame de la Salabière as they wish. Personally, I would just as soon credit the Chinese with being the first to mix milk with their tea, given the age-old recipe for tea-and-rice soup with sour yak milk—even if Yu Lu did consider it slop-water of a ditch.

Despite Garway's and others' enthusiastic encomia on the health benefits of tea, the directors of the East India Company declined to import any tea from the Far East, even though they themselves were drinking the stuff at company meetings. They procured their tea from a nearby coffeehouse keeper—and even though Catherine of Braganza, King Charles II's bride, had in 1662 arrived from Portugal with a trunkload of tea for her own habit. It wasn't until 1668 that the directors finally ordered "100 lb. waight of the best tey that you can get" from company representatives in Bantam in the Dutch East Indies. The rest, as they say, is history. Shortly thereafter, George, Lord Berkeley, commissioned a teapot and had it inscribed

This silver tea Pott was presented to the Com^{ttee} of the East India Company by the Right Hono^e George Ld Berkeley of Berkeley Castle. A member of that Honourable and worthy Society and A true hearty Lover of them. 1670

Shape of George Berkeley's silver teapot, Presented to the East India Company in 1670. Unlike any Chinese porcelain or Yixing pot of the time and in fact rather Gothic looking; one wonders what, precisely, in the silversmith's shop Berkeley pointed at when ordering it. John Bedford, author of *Talking about Teapots*, thinks the prototype was a delftware teapot of decidedly coffeepot shape made in Holland about the same time. Berkeley's teapot can be seen at the Victoria and Albert Museum, London.

The teapot is now in the Victoria and Albert Museum in London, where it enjoys the distinction of being the first teapot made in England. I like to imagine Lord Berkeley year after year nudging his fellow directors to import tea, and rewarding them with the teapot when they finally did, although I confess that's stretching history to the breaking point.

According to Sam Twining, in his book *My Cup of Tea: The Story of the World's Most Popular Beverage*, the East India Company's first order of tea in 1668 amounted to 143.5 pounds. In 1678 the company imported 4,713 pounds; in 1700, 20,000 pounds; and in 1721, 1 million pounds. To say that tea caught on is an understatement provocative of hilarity. But tea was not cheap; Stephen Twining in 2003 estimated that today's package of Twining's 25 teabags would have sold for the equivalent of $100.00 in 1706. Only the aristocracy could afford tea at those prices, and the lady of the house kept hers under lock and key so the servants wouldn't steal it.

Among the earliest porcelain teapots shipped to Europe were pear-shaped pots with straight spouts. They were called East India pots or pots from the East Indies. Straight spouts were sought after in the days before strainers at the base of the spout; you could clean them out more easily than swan-necked spouts when they clogged with tea leaves. But the earliest teapots common in shipments to Europe were swan-necked pots, with round, squat bodies; shallow, dome covers; and square, overhead handles. Some lovely examples of this type were salvaged by Captain Michael Hatcher in 1983–1984 from a Chinese trading vessel sunk in 1643–1646 off the islands and reefs of the Lingga archipelago south of Singapore, on its way to Batavia. (Sometimes called the Hatcher Junk, the vessel's cargo was auctioned in Amsterdam in 1984 by Christie's, which later sold the sensational Nanking cargo of the *Geldermalsen*.)

By 1709 enough people in England were drinking tea that one East India Company order stipulated "40 tons of Chinaware" including 50,000 teacups and saucers and 5,000 "teapots with straight spouts."

Blue and White Teapots

These early porcelain teapots—straight-spouted or swan-necked—were the blue and white *qinghua* wares we so immediately associate with China. This type of porcelain is called "underglaze blue hard-paste porcelain" by museums and serious antiques dealers. The porcelain imported to England by the East Indiamen was divided into two groups: official imports of the East India Company, and officially permitted private trade. The private trade porcelain tended to be of a far higher quality and more unique in design than the East India Company bulk purchases. The bulk purchases—which were often called ballast ware because they could be stored below the waterline on the ship, unlike tea, which would be ruined if it got wet—were sold at auction and were the true original export porcelain, at least as far as the Chinese were concerned.

Even though the first silver English teapot appeared on the London scene in 1670, and the English aristocracy were great collectors of plate, with display cabinet after display cabinet in their townhouses and country estates to showcase the stuff, British tea drinkers did not rush out to commission silver teapots, at least not at first. People who at the turn of the 18th century were happily plunking down the equivalent of $100.00 for a quantity of tea comparable to that in a modern Twining's box of tea bags preferred to brew their tea in Chinese porcelain and *zisha* teapots. We know this because they had family portraits painted showing themselves seated around their tea tables—complete with these same Chinese teapots, bowls, saucers, and the various other items that came to constitute the *au courant* tea-drinker's *equipage*.

Imari, *Famille Verte,* and *Famille Rose*

Between the fall of the Ming dynasty (1644) and the firm establishment of the Qing, political unrest disrupted the porcelain factories at Jingdezhen. Europeans turned to Japanese wares painted in underglaze blue, overglaze iron red, and gold to fill the gap. These Japanese wares, called Imari, then became a market force the Chinese had to reckon with once they were back in business. Color suddenly became very big. First came a luminous palette of translucent enamels, dominated by shades of green, called by the French *famille verte*. Then, aided by European Jesuit priests who knew a thing or two about paint technology, the Chinese were able to produce an Imari-like style of their own, called Chinese Imari to distinguish it from its Japanese prototype. During the 1720s, Chinese ceramists—again, aided by the Jesuits—experimented with an overglaze rose enamel made from chloride of gold; this palette was called *fen-cai* (foreign color) by the Chinese and *famille rose* by the French, and was exported by the 1730s.

Jean McClure Mudge, writing in *Chinese Export Porcelain in North America*, probably has the best explanation of what *famille rose* is and why it had such an important impact on the Chinese export trade:

"The introduction of the rose palette was more than the addition of one color and its hues. It added a new range in the Chinese painter's palette. Technically, the gold red, as the Chinese translate it today to distinguish it from copper-red, was combined with a white oxide of arsenic and fired in a low-temperature kiln. The white not only gave a spectrum of rose hues from deep ruby to the palest pink but could be combined with enamels of any color, thus making 'soft' or 'pale' colors—pastels."

Moreover, the emperor Qianlong (1736–1795) liked wares painted with the new colors better than the traditional blue and white. The potters at Jingdezhen went

***Famille Rose* teapot.** Qianlong Seal & Period (1736–1795). Ovid shaped teapot with a high-domed lid and ear-shaped handle, with a bent and curving spout. Painted on both sides with a scene of ten children at play under a gnarled pine tree and rockwork setting, symbolizing longevity. The Chinese characters (four sets) on the lid are "double happiness." Base and interior painted in a pale turquoise color, with the Qianlong seal in red. Excellent condition with minor wear; no chips, cracks, or repairs. Size: 6³/₄" high (including lid) x 7¹/₂ (from spout to end of handle). $1,200.00 in 2003. Photo courtesy Asia House.

into overdrive to supply the court with *famille rose* porcelain. Possibly because the emperor liked it, *famille rose* was consistently a very high-quality product that would be unsurpassed in later periods.

According to Geoffrey Godden (*Sotheby's Concise Encyclopedia of Porcelain*), one interesting thing about early (before 1740) Chinese teapots is that the glaze was trimmed away from both the filling aperture and the inside flange of the teapot lid. This allowed the teapots to be fired with their lids on, without the lids becoming glued to the pots by the glaze. At the same time, firing both lids and pots together ensured a snug-fitting teapot lid. There is another interesting feature of Chinese-made teapots: Many early pots do not have strainer holes at the base of the spout, but when strainer holes are present, you can see that they were crudely punched into the pot from the outside, causing flaking of the glaze around the holes. This is one way to tell a Chinese-made from a European- or American-made teapot; even modern Chinese teapots are still made this way.

As I have already noted, teapots that have survived from the 1700s and early 1800s were made to brew Chinese tea, some of which was very large-leafed, so the strainer holes needed to be larger than those in more modern teapots. The larger the strainer holes, the fewer of them you would need to pour the tea. Chinese teapots from the 1700s and 1800s may therefore have only three holes. By the late 19th century most tea imported into England was Indian and processed by machine into smaller pieces. Teapots made in England for Indian tea required more and smaller holes, and the Chinese, always happy to copy a profitable design (even if it was to be used by the competition), began to make teapots with more and smaller holes, too.

Nanking, Canton, Rose Medallion, and Fitzhugh Teapots

In the latter part of the 20th century, many Chinese teapots from the 1600s and 1700s came to light in the form of salvaged cargoes of shipwrecks; I have already mentioned the Hatcher Junk and the Nanking cargo of the *Geldermalsen* auctioned by Christie's in Amsterdam in 1986. The *Geldermalsen* sank in January 1752 off the islands and reefs of the Lingga archipelago south of Singapore, bequeathing us a fabulous time capsule of teapots. The auction catalog lists four groups of them: bullet-shaped teapots in blue and white; bullet-shaped teapots in enamels; globular teapots in blue and enamels; and Yixing stoneware teapots. All date from about 1750.

Christie's decision to promote the cargo as "Nanking," however, was infelicitous. Colin Sheaf defended that decision in the catalog's introduction, explaining that

" . . . this type of export blue and white porcelain, and most particularly those pieces with elaborate underglaze blue border patterns, has been called 'Nanking' or 'Nankeen' since it began to appear in trade advertisements and auction catalogs in the 1760s. Western wholesalers and retailers incorrectly believed that these typical fine-quality ceramics for the export trade were made at Nanking. In fact, almost all were potted at the famous porcelain city of Jingdezhen in Jiangxi Province."

Unfortunately, during the 234 years between the sinking of the *Geldermalsen* and the sale of its cargo in 1986,

Chinese Export Nanking Teapot, ca. 1736–1795. Drum shape with gilding and crossed strap handles joined to the body amongst clusters of vines and berries. Characteristic island and riverscape scene, but with unusual figure on a bridge and carrying an umbrella. Meticulously painted latticework borders most often associated with Nanking; an attractive variation combines butterflies in flight, split pomegranates, and flowering branches, much in the style Fitzhugh. While frequently applied by decorators in Canton, gilding was sometimes the work of English or American craftspersons. Excellent condition, with two small minor flakes on the inside of the bottom rim. Size: 9¹/₂" length (from tip of spout to end of handle) x 5" Dia. of base. $1,500.00 in 2003. Photo courtesy Asia House.

Nanking as a ceramics term had come to designate something extremely specific: wares painted with a geometric lattice and spear-and-post border; consistently well potted and of aesthetically fine and delicate quality; often gilded on rims, spouts, handles, and other areas; and produced on special-order only—i.e., private trade porcelain. This was not the right term for the basic everyday porcelain shipped as high-quality ballast aboard the *Geldermalsen*: generic blue and white, utilitarian, and much more coarsely potted than what most modern-day collectors of Chinese export porcelain mean when they say "Nanking."

The bane of any collector is terminology. Which brings us to yet another confusion: *Canton ware*. In America, *Canton* designates underglaze blue and white ware of a standardized pattern of landscapes or coastal village scenes with teahouses, arched bridges, willow trees, meandering streams and distant mountains, bordered with latticework and wavy or scalloped lines called *clouds*. Canton ware was shipped as ballast and generally dates from the late 18th to late 19th century. In Europe, *Canton* is used to describe a colorful flower-and-figures pattern with a gilded, green-scrolled background—what Americans know as *Rose Medallion*.

Fitzhugh is a pattern dating from the late 18th century. The pattern consists of a central medallion and four surrounding panels depicting flowers, pomegranates, butterflies, and other Chinese motifs, with a repeating border design of more flowers, pomegranates, and butterflies, incorporated into a Greek key fret border. Where the name Fitzhugh came from originally is anybody's guess; one reputable scholar has suggested—one can only imagine with irony—that it's a corruption of Foochow, the name of a city in southeastern China. In any case, the term is not used in Great Britain or Europe.

Canton is always blue and white; Fitzhugh comes in a variety of colors. Nanking is usually blue and white, but it may be orange or green. Orange Nanking is rare; green Nanking is even rarer. Canton teapots may be square (somewhat rare), drum shape, lighthouse shape, or sencer (square-ish with four feet) shape.

If you're about to become passionate about Chinese-export-porcelain teapots, you need to know that *Chinese export porcelain* is a fairly recent bit of nomenclature. Variously at times in the past, this ware has been called *India Company china; chine de commande* (as we have seen, not all of it was *de commande*); and, most unhappily of all, *Oriental Lowestoft*, a designation that persisted for more than a hundred years despite being proved wrong time after time again. *Chinese export porcelain* is generally not used to describe 20th-century wares, even if they are Chinese, made for foreign markets, and porcelain.

By the end of the 19th century, interest in new Chinese export porcelain had pretty much sputtered out both in Europe and in the United States. But at the same time, collectors became interested in earlier pieces. In the 1950s there was a flurry of serious scholarship, and since then some excellent books on Chinese export have been published. Eighteenth- and early-19th-century pottery is now desirable among the old-money crowd and glitterati (creamware is especially popular), so Chinese export porcelain is a comparative bargain.

Prices for teapots vary, depending on age, condition, uniqueness of design, datability, and provenance. At this writing, an average of prices listed for Canton teapots on a reputable Web site was $697.50, with the highest price

Coconut teapot with wood handle and spout. Recently purchased in Taiwan. Made from an actual coconut, the pot playfully tweaks Asia's long-established prominence in all things tea.

$1,210.00 and the lowest $330.00; the earliest sale listed was 1996 and the most recent 2002.

The Japanese Tea Ceremony

"In the fifteenth century," writes Okakura Kakuzo in *The Book of Tea*, "Japan ennobled tea into a religion of estheticism—Teaism."

Remember Bodhidharma, who tore off his eyelids, threw them on the ground, and witnessed a tea bush grow from them? Known in Japan as Daruma, he is considered the founder of the Dhyan, or Zen, sect of Buddhism. Zen priests are believed to have originally brought tea to Japan, and along with it the elaborate ceremony of whipped tea as it was drunk in China during the Sung dynasty (960–1368). Abbot Yeisai (sometimes called Yeisai-zenji or Eisai-zenji), Japan's "Father of Tea," did much to promote the cultivation and drinking of it during the last decade of the tenth century and early years of the eleventh. Gradually, tea drinking extended from the priests and religious to the laity, and as William Ukers tells us in *All about Tea*, the sacred beverage "became an excuse for congenial gatherings of friends and retainers, for learned or religious discourse, for political purposes, and later, in *Cha-no-yu*, it became an esthetic rite."

Cha-no-yu means "hot water tea." The first ceremonies were held in temple groves, where the harmony of nature became an intricate part of the ritual. Later when *cha-no-yu* became popular in towns, an attempt was made to re-create natural surroundings by celebrating the ritual in a little room set aside for that purpose or a teahouse surrounded by gardens. Senno Rikyu, who founded the most popular school of *cha-no-yu*, Ukers continues, "forbade frivolous conversation in the tearoom, and demanded that the simplest movements be performed according to strict rules of ceremony and a prescribed decorum. A subtle philosophy lay behind it all . . . known to the Japanese as 'Teaism.'"

Teaism is a ritualistic system founded on devotion to what is beautiful in life: love of nature, simplicity, and tolerance. The tea ceremony celebrates the Zen concepts of *wabi* and *sabi* (solitariness, being left behind, loss of self), *wa* (harmony), *kei* (awe), *sei* (purity), and *jaku* (quiet). The Japanese speak of a person who is incapable of appreciating the finer things in life as having "no tea in him," and of the aesthete as having "too much tea." Okakura elaborates:

"When we consider how small after all the cup of human enjoyment is, how soon overflowed with tears, how easily drained to the dregs in our quenchless thirst for infinity, we shall not blame ourselves for making so much of the teacup. Mankind has done worse. In the worship of Bacchus we have sacrificed too freely; and we have even transfigured the gory image of Mars. Why not consecrate ourselves to the queen of the Camelias, and revel in the warm stream of sympathy that flows from her altar? In the liquid amber within the ivory-porcelain, the initiated may touch the sweet reticence of Confucius, the piquancy of Lao-tse, and the ethereal aroma of Sakyamuni himself."

The earliest rules for *cha-no-yu* were promulgated during the time of the shogun Yoshimasa (1443–1473), who added to his palace the first nine-by-nine-foot tearoom, astonishingly still in existence today and open to visitors at the *Ginkaku-ji* in Kyoto. A century later, Senno Rikyu felt these rules needed revising. He set them down in writing; here they are quoted from Ukers:

1. As soon as the guests are assembled in the waiting room, they announce themselves by knocking on a wooden gong.

2. It is important on entering this ceremony to have not only a clean face and hands, but chiefly a clean heart.

3. The host must meet his guests and conduct them in. If, on account of the host's poverty, he cannot give them tea and necessaries for the ceremony, or if the eatables be tasteless, or even if the trees and rocks do not please him, the guest can leave at once.

4. As soon as the water makes a sound like a wind in the fir trees, and the bell rings, the guests should return from the waiting room, for bad would it be to forget the right moment for the water and the fire.

5. It is forbidden, since long ago, to speak in or out of the house of anything worldly. In this category comes political conversation, and especially scandal. The only thing is the Tea and the Tea Societies.

6. No guest or host may, in any true, pure meeting, flatter either by word or deed.

7. A meeting may not last longer than two hours (Japanese)— four hours European time.

Notice: Let the time pass by in talking about these rules and maxims. The Tea Societies recognize no difference of social standing, but permit free intercourse between high and low.

Written in the 12th year of Tensho (1584), and on the 9th day of the 9th month.

If you are a teapot enthusiast who is drawn to the ceremonial and you read the above, you may be wondering what kind of teapot is used for *cha-no-yu*, and where you can buy one. Brace yourself: there is no tea-ceremony teapot, at least not in the traditional Japanese tea ceremony (the Chinese tea ceremony does incorporate use of teapots). A traditional Japanese tea ceremony is conducted with *matsu-cha* (powdered tea), which is whisked in a bowl, not brewed in a pot—because the Zen priests who originally brought the tea ceremony to Japan left China during the Sung dynasty, long before the invention of teapots.

Somehow thereafter the Chinese and Japanese failed to compare tea notes. Despite established trade routes between the two countries, it never occurred to early Ming dynasty tea drinkers in China, weeping and wailing and beating their breasts because no one knew anymore what a tea whisk looked like, to ask their Japanese neigh-

Japanese tetsubin, 21st century.
Originally used to boil water for the tea ceremony, this classical teakettle in its modern incarnation may come with a stainless mesh infuser for brewing loose tea. Available at this writing for $85.00 at T Salon and T Emporium, 1-888-NYCTEAS.

bors. Nor did the Japanese think to find out from the Chinese if anything interesting had happened in Chinese tea circles in oh-why-don't-we-say the last couple hundred years. One likes to think that Rikyu, who died in 1591, might have been intrigued by early teapots and leaf tea. But perhaps not.

While there was no teapot per se involved in the Japanese tea ceremony, the *tetsubin* teakettle could and eventually did come to play a role. *Cha-no-yu* called for hot water to be ladled from a *cha-gama*, a relatively large amphora-like vessel without a spout. As more and more common people began to drink tea, however, and after the Japanese literati in the 17th century revolted against the formality of *cha-no-yu* (then favored by the ruling class), teakettles came into use. Made of cast iron, they were used as kettles to heat water; later, when leaf tea finally became popular in Japan, they could be used to brew tea as well.

Modern *tetsubin* often feature removable stainless-steel infusing baskets, so when tea is finished steeping, the basket can be removed. Some *tetsubin* owners have two kettles—one to brew the tea while the second is warming; when the tea finishes brewing in the first, they pour out the warming water from the second and decant the tea into it. The two prefectures best known for *tetsubin* are Iwate, which is considered to produce the best designs and quality at a reasonable price, and Yamagata, which is best known for the handmade *tetsubin* and *cha-gama* still used by tea ceremony masters.

Many people believe that water heated in a cast-iron *tetsubin* not only improves the taste of tea, but has added health benefits. If you're of this school of thought, make sure when you buy or order your *tetsubin* that the interior has not been coated with enamel to help prevent rust.

While the steeping of leaf tea came late to Japan—according to Okakura Kakuzo, not until the middle 1600s—there are many extant examples of "pouring vessels" or spouted pots from Japan that date from much earlier. Like Chinese ewers and wine pots, they may or may not have been used to brew tea but were on the scene when people decided they needed a suitable pot for steeping. One Japanese stoneware spouted pot in the Victoria and Albert Museum in London, for example, dates from the Momoyama period (1573–1615); it has cute little feet, a recessed lid, and overhead handle, and is what might be called a somewhat squashed bullet or globular shape—very teapot-like.

Imari Teapots

About the same time that steeped tea was coming into use in Japan, a number of other things were happening. While China was in a state of semi–civil war as outgoing Ming dynasty loyalists and incoming Qing dynasty supporters duked it out, Japan enjoyed a newfound peace ushered in by Shogun Tokugawa Ieyasu when he effected the unification of Japan in 1603. By the mid-17th century, the samurai warrior class, essentially now unemployed, was busying itself with literature, philosophy, and tea ceremonies. The increase in tea ceremony appreciation meant a boom in tea ceremony wares, happily supplied by Japanese pottery and porcelain makers. The potting industry, already enjoying a renaissance of technology and design largely set into motion by an influx of talented Korean ceramists during Ieyasu's reign, discovered how to make porcelain sometime around 1600. A few decades later they developed a new overglaze technique that allowed them to paint the porcelain with polychrome. While the exact date and inventor of this method has been lost in the fog of history, legend credits craftsman Sakaida Kakiemon I.

We do know that polychrome overglaze enamelware was probably first produced in the 1640s; that this type of ceramic was called *nishiki-de* ("brocaded") by a monk writing in his tea diary in 1652; and that the Dutch, desperate to fill orders as the porcelain industry ground to a halt in China, in 1657 shipped the new Japanese blue-red-and-gold porcelain wares instead. Europeans, generally clueless as to what went on in China and Japan beyond the strictly defined port areas Barbarians were allowed to trade in, named the new wares *Imari* after the Japanese port from which they were shipped.

With its vivid red, blue, and gold palette, Imari porcelain created a sensation among European buyers accustomed to blue and white Chinese wares. The Dutch East India Company, which in 1656 had ordered 4,149 pieces, in 1659 upped the number to 64,866. I think it's safe to assume that among these orders would have been teapots; the Dutch East India Company, unlike its English counterpart, had been importing tea since the 1630s and had specially ordered blue and white pots to brew it in from Jingdezhen as early as 1639.

Catalogued in modern museum and private collections as wine pots, ewers, spouted pots, and pouring vessels, extant examples of these early "East India pots" tend to fly under the radar of teapot collectors. But they're out there if you want to see them. (I'm assuming that you not only want to buy, but want to look and learn as well.) While private collections are of course inaccessible to the viewing public, from time to time entire lots of stuff go on sale at Christie's or Sotheby's, or are generously loaned by their owners to museums.

One such exhibition, "Imari: Japanese Porcelains for European Palaces," drawn from the extensive collection of Freda and Ralph Lupin, was mounted by the New Orleans Museum of Art in the late 1990s. I missed the show, but I was able to lay hands on the fabulous catalog written by Lisa Rotando-McCord at the New York Public Library. In it were pictured a late-17th-century Imari covered pouring vessel, cylindrical in shape with a loop handle, long spout, and slightly domed shallow cover; an Imari wine pot, ca. 1700, with an overhead handle, long slit spout, and shallow domed cover; and five Imari teapots from the same time period, these last globular in shape with straight or nearly straight spouts. The early Imari colors were a delight to behold, and the hour I spent perusing the book was an escape from the world—a Teaism experience if ever there was one.

The word *Imari* and related nomenclature present another experience of thrashing through the thicket of obscure, ambiguous, and confusing terminology. Porcelain shipped from the port of Imari in the 17th century for the most part was manufactured in the nearby Japanese town of Arita and its environs and comprises two types: *sometsuke* (what the Japanese called blue and white) and polychrome (many colors). Polychrome came in two styles: *nishiki-de* ("brocaded"), where basically the entire field was lavishly painted, leaving little or no white space; and *Kakiemon*, with delicate designs painted on a white background with lots of white showing. Kakiemon is named after the legendary inventor of polychrome overglaze enamel.

When the Chinese copied Japanese polychrome styles, their wares were also, unfortunately, called Imari, now often *Chinese Imari* to distinguish it from Japanese. Arita today continues its long tradition of pottery and porcelain production; wares produced there are called *aritayaki* by the Japanese. *Imari* as applicable to ceramics made since 1912 narrowly describes porcelain painted in brocade style. Arita-area exports from the time before exports to Europe may be called *Shoki-Imari* or *Ko-Imari;* but *Ko-Imari* may also mean antique as opposed to modern.

Imari has been in and out of fashion over the years; Queen Mary II of England (of William and Mary), filled her palaces to overflowing with it at the end of the 17th century. It was quite the rage in Europe until the mid-18th century. The new porcelain factories in Germany, France, and England copied it. During the mid- to late 19th century there was a revival of interest in this porcelain, which continued into the early 20th. Interest waned in the 1930s, but private collection exhibitions in England's great houses reawakened it in the 1980s.

Japanese Imari teapots from the early 18th century can command prices beyond the pocketbook of ordinary collectors—a Japanese teapot in the form of a seated *bijin* painted in typical Imari palette, ca. 1700, recently sold for about $10,300—but others often sell in the low four figures, for example a ca. 1760 5-inch-high teapot that according to *www.kovels.com* went for $1,610.00 in 1997. An 18th-century Imari ribbed melon-shaped teapot went for $850.00 in 1996, also according to *www.kovels.com*. Modern Imari teapots decorated in old styles are readily available for less than a hundred dollars.

In the buyer-beware department, if it says Imari on the bottom, it's mid-to-late-20th-century giftware. Authentic, antique Japanese Imari is unmarked, other than an occasional benevolent sentiment, for example "good luck."

Nabeshima and Hirado

Originally, Nabeshima and Hirado were private kilns operated by the princely families of Nabeshima and Matsura, producing ceramic wares only for family use and what are called presentation pieces: gifts for the lords to give other lords, shoguns, and the emperor. These pieces were highly important in a culture with an elaborate and complicated tradition of gift-giving. Gifts for the emperor had to be the most exquisite and the best quality possible, setting a very high standard of achievement. The Nabeshima kilns went public in the 19th century, as did those of Hirado, making these wares available to the buying consumer for the first time.

Hirado teapots often come in the form of jolly fat figures with their bellies protruding out from under their robes; these may be genuine antiques or modern copies of old styles. Other Hirado teapots may be more conventionally shaped, like one underglaze blue and white late-Meiji–early-Taisha (1910s–1920s) pot depicting scholars playing the game of Go on a low table. Delicately potted and in perfect condition, it recently sold for $300.00. Hirado, by the way, is at the moment "underestimated and considered a good buy," according to expert Julian Critchley.

Satsuma

Satsuma earthenware seems to be an acquired taste; some people collect nothing but, while experts often sniff that it is "not to be taken seriously" or is "grossly overdecorated." If you do a Google search for "Satsuma teapot," you will see immediately a very wide variety, from sparely decorated, Yixing-like teapots to pots so lavishly and gaudily painted, they glow more than neon. Clearly there's something in Satsuma ware for every taste. Prices range anywhere from a luridly decorated 1890 Satsuma teapot selling for $275.00 to an exuberantly painted $5,500.00 teapot by master Satsuma artist Yabu Meizan. If you like Satsuma, don't be deterred by the not-to-be-taken-seriously quotient; one generation's not-to-be-taken-seriously often becomes the next generation's hot must-have collectible.

Raku and Banko

During the reign of Hideyoshi, a Korean potter developed a kind of earthenware fired at a very low temperature on a hearth. The pottery was painted with a treacly glaze that fused at the same temperature. *Temmoku* (tea bowls) made from it were breathtakingly simple and primitive, and they caught the eye of Hideyoshi, who awarded the potter a gold seal engraved with the word *raku* ("enjoyment" or "being well-chosen"). Later, an amateur potter, Gozaemon Numanami(1736–1795), produced an eclectic style of raku wares, incorporating ideas from Satsuma, Ming polychrome porcelain, and Dutch delft. Gozaemon took the *nom d'artiste* Banko, meaning "Ever-Enduring." During the 19th century, Yusetsu Mori (1808–1882) purchased the formulas from Banko's grandson; his wares are sometimes called *Banko II* or *Yusetsu Banko* to distinguish it from *Ko-Banko* (Old Banko). Eventually, Banko earthenware came to be copied enthusiastically by Japanese potters everywhere. Recently Banko teapots have become very popular among collectors; early examples are rare, but pots from the late 19th century turn up from time to time. More readily available are 20th-century Banko teapots. Often whimsical in shape, style, and color, these modern teapots show how the style, technique, choice of clay, and quality of Banko ware have evolved over time.

Modern Japanese Teapots

Two types of modern Japanese teapots are *dobin* and *kyushu*, the former a large teapot, conventional in shape, that is capable of serving several people; the latter a

Japanese pink lustreware teapot, ca. 1920s. Marked on the bottom "2/3998." Strainer at base of spout. Teapot courtesy Miriam Novalle, T Salon and T Emporium.

smaller, more individual serving–size with a straight handle attached at right angles to the spout. Both *dobin* and *kyushu* are generally available by mail order from Web sites catering to serious tea drinkers.

The export of Japanese ceramics to foreign marketplaces, particularly to the United States and Europe, has become so well established in the last century that it is very nearly cliché. Any kind of teapot imaginable was and is had from Japan. Many ceramics are imported into the West by the Otagiri company, which specializes in tableware designed in America but manufactured in Japan. In 1960 a former Otagiri designer, a Mr. Floyd, left to form Fitz and Floyd, now marketers of a very popular line of miniature teapots in addition to brightly colored and cheerful full-size pots. All the favorite themes are revisited: jolly fat figures with protruding bellies, charming animals, fruits and flowers, characters from children's stories. Edward Bramah perhaps sums it up best: "Not only do the creatures manage to be appealing without excessive cuteness but there are sometimes touches of real wit. And all these teapots will pour."

A popular design among collectors has been Geisha Girl porcelain, so named because it is decorated with women wearing kimonos. Manufactured beginning in the 1920s and designed for the export market, and for sale to servicemen and tourists, Geisha Girl porcelain was originally quite inexpensive. Often, in fact, it was retailed at dime stores or given away as premiums. According to

Traditional gaiwan tea bowl. Many Chinese still brew tea in a bowl, not a teapot. To drink, one holds the lid over the top except for a tiny space along the edge of the rim; this method strains the tea. Gaiwan courtesy of Miriam Novalle, T Salon & T Emporium.

Jay Moore, who writes a column on antiques for the *Tampa Tribune*, there were at least 150 makers of Geisha Girl porcelain that produced a minimum of 300 pattern variations in hundreds of forms. "Production came to a virtual halt during the occupation and was revived, for a brief period, in the 1980s," Moore wrote recently. "The new pieces have gold decorations on the red-orange borders and are smooth and white compared with the old items, which are rough and gray by comparison."

Noritake porcelain, first produced in 1904 in Nagoya, Japan, is another popular collectible, exported to every country on the face of the globe. If it has been imported directly into the United States, it will be marked on the bottom either "Made in Japan" or "Nippon." Pieces imported by countries without country-of-origin regulations, however, are usually unmarked. There are hundreds of patterns; see Aimee Neff Alden's *Collector's Encyclopedia of Early Noritake*.

European Yixing Copies: Red Teapots

The first teapots to come to Europe were Yixing teapots, imported during the 17th century by the officers and crews of the East India Company as officially sanctioned private trade. The first ceramic teapots made in Europe were copies of the Yixing pots.

Until recently, this link was poorly understood, mostly because the Chinese history of teapots was inaccessible to

Dutch redware teapot. By Ary de Milde, ca. late 17th or early 18th century. This globe-shaped pot, with a circular squat base, conical spout, lateral ear-shaped handle, and dome-shaped lid (slightly flat in its upper part), was a popular model among late-17th-century potters in Delft, Holland. Modeled on a Yixing original. Photo courtesy Historisch Museum het Burgerweeshuis, Arnhem, The Netherlands, on loan from the I.C.N., Amsterdam.

Western readers. Philip Miller and Michael Berthoud, whose *An Anthology of British Teapots* was published in 1985, in particular lamented the lack of materials in English; undoubtedly they would have been heartened to see K.S. Lo's book, *The Stonewares of Yixing*, published a year after *Anthology*. In 1990 the Hong Kong Museum came out with *The Art of the Yixing Potter*; that was followed in 2000 by Patrice Valfré's *Yixing: Des Théières pour l'Europe*.

These books did much to illuminate teapot history for Westerners. Since the publication of their book, many of Miller's and Berthoud's time-honored theorems have been disproved, the most striking example being: "The teapot as a vessel specifically designed for the brewing of the beverage was unknown in the Orient where tea was individually brewed in tea bowls." Westerners now know that while many Chinese brewed tea in bowls, as some still do—witness my sister-in-law's mother, Mama Hu, who drank tea from sunrise to sundown every day of the year but used a teapot only to add hot water to the leaves in her traditional *gaiwan* tea bowl—Yixing teapots predate the first Western teapots by more than one hundred and fifty years. Yet many, many teapot books and Web sites continue to repeat the old myth that Westerners invented the teapot. Don't believe it.

The Dutch were the first Europeans to catch the tea bug, and by the mid-17th century they were drinking gallons of

Shape of Meissen teapot, ca. 1715–1720. Johann Friedrich Böttger achieved a red stoneware of unusual hardness in 1708. The ware could be polished until the surface was as shiny as jasper, after which he named it. For twenty years teapots of this material were produced by the Meissen factory. One of this shape, with silver-gilt mounts and chain, can be seen at the Getty Museum, or you may view a photo on the museum's Web site at www.getty.edu/art/collections/bio/a1219-1.html.

the stuff, right about the time the first coffeehouses in London were opening. The pottery industry in Delft at that time was busy turning out *gallyware* (the tin-glazed, blue and white earthenware we now call delft), but had in the past produced various red stonewares, and were happy to accommodate the new demand for teapots using Yixing pots as prototypes. Local red wares were of course not the same as Yixing, however, and soon the race was on to find a formula that would most successfully approximate *red porcelain,* as Yixing was called at the time.

Whether Ary de Milde was the first to make a delft red stoneware teapot is still a topic of scholarly speculation; certainly, his pots are among the oldest to survive to the present. De Milde, who apparently liked to call himself Mr. Tea Pot Man, was also one of the most prolific potters of his day. His oval sigillated mark of a running fox seemingly appears on the underside of every pot in Holland. His 1679 application in partnership with Sammuel von Eenhoom, here as quoted by Valfré, reads as follows:

"We, associates, have discovered production techniques which make it possible for us to copy the teapots from the East Indies. We request permission to produce these pots for fifteen years and to be the only ones to market them."

A year earlier, Lambertus Cleffus, another master potter at Delft, had advertised red teapots, claiming to have been making them since 1672. According to Ukers, John Dwight of Fulham made the first ceramic teapot in England, also in 1672, a hard-fired red stoneware pot modeled on Yixing pots. But Ary de Milde is generally credited with having made the first European ceramic teapot, and extant pots of his making date to ca. 1670–1680.

According to Valfré, the Delft potters produced replica Yixing teapots from about 1675 to 1725, reaching peak production about 1700.

Soft-Paste Porcelain and Flying Teapots

While it was relatively easy to approximate the Yixing stonewares, European potters at the same time were desperate to duplicate Chinese porcelain. Soft-paste porcelain, so called because it was made with glass-like materials mixed with clay that when fired never quite achieved the hardness of Asian-made porcelain, was produced by various factories in Italy, Spain, and Holland as early as the late 16th century. The Medicis in particular spent a great deal of money to fund the search for the elusive hard-paste formula, using white clay suspended in a glass-like quartz silica. But the results never quite met expectations.

So-called *Medici porcelain* is sometimes considered the first European porcelain despite the fact that it was only soft-paste. Difficult to work with and more fragile when finished than hard-paste, soft-paste was nonetheless much warmer and richer in appearance than contemporary pottery or even majolica. At the end of the 16th century, soft-paste's creamy white color was amenable to decoration with a broader range of colors than other forms of pottery.

In England in the late 16th century, soft-paste wares were made of various mixtures of ground-up glass, bone, lime ash, phosphatic (bone), and steatitic (soapstone). By the 1740s several potteries were producing soft-paste porcelain teapots. Chelsea (1745–1784) specialized in Chinoiserie-painted teapots, and teapots left white (copied from the German porcelain factories, which themselves had copied Chinese originals). Bow (ca. 1744–1776) called it-self "New Canton" and produced a soft-paste porcelain containing bone ash; lovely teapots of this type looked exactly like their Chinese-porcelain prototypes. William Duesbury of Derby bought out the Chelsea factory in 1770, and he acquired the Bow molds when Bow closed. The Chelsea operation later became Royal Crown Derby. Worcester was established in 1751, copying Japanese Kakiemon and Imari designs at first, later the lavishly florid Sèvres patterns. Lowestoft made Chinese-style teapots in underglaze blue or enamels; oddly, these pots bore marks copied from Meissen and Worcester just as often as not.

The fragility of soft-paste teapots often caused the pots to explode when boiling water was poured into them, prob-ably not very funny to people at the time but adding a cer-tain note of hilarity to historical accounts. From these exploding soft-paste teapots comes the sobriquet "flying teapot." According to Sam Twining, ninth-generation scion of the famous tea family, customers were advised to warm their teapots gradually before pouring in boiling water. "It is thought that tea drinkers would also put a little milk into their tea bowls to avoid them shatter-ing," he writes in *My Cup of Tea: The Story of the World's Most Popular Beverage*. "The legendary origin of 'MIF'— milk in first! In fact there are records of milk in tea much earlier..." Pouring milk into the bowl would hardly solve the flying-pot problem, but the legend continues to charm.

To pursue the milk question briefly, we have already seen that the Chinese recommended adding milk to some of their tea-as-medicine recipes, although it may have been of the sour-yak-milk variety. In European circles, milk seems to have been offered with tea from the early 1700s; as Twining points out, in some households there was a designated pitcher for it. "But milk was not taken seriously," he adds, "until the pungent, malty teas of Assam, India, started entering Britain in 1839."

A final note on soft-paste porcelain teapots: few have survived to today. Apparently most of them flew. Eighteenth-century Bow, Chelsea, Worcester, and Lowe-stoft teapots do turn up from time to time at auctions of fine antiques, but not frequently. If you fantasize about snagging a teapot at a garage sale for $25.00, then going on the *Antiques Roadshow* and finding out it's worth thousands . . . an English soft-paste teapot from the mid-18th century might fit the bill.

Böttger, European Hard-Paste Porcelain, and Meissen

So eager were the rulers of Europe in the early 1700s to discover the secret of porcelain manufacture that not one but two of them threatened to kidnap alchemist Johann Friedrich Böttger, alleged to be able to turn silver into gold. Elector Friederich Augustus I of Saxony (later King Augustus II the Strong of Poland) had Böttger arrested when he fled across the Saxony border. Augustus, a rabid collector of porcelain, would go on to become famous for exchanging a regiment of dragoons (600 armed cavalry) for 151 pieces of porcelain with Friedrich Wilhelm I of Prussia. It was Augustus who succinctly defined *Sammelleidenschaft* ("collecting-affliction-passion"):

"Don't you realize that it's the same for porcelain as it is for oranges, I mean that if you suffer from either one sickness or the other, you can never get enough of them, on the contrary, one just craves for more."

Böttger must have realized what he was up against. Effectively under house arrest, he set about finding the hard-paste formula in earnest.

Because both red stoneware of the Yixing prototype and Chinese wares from Jingdezhen were considered porcelain by the Europeans, Böttger first set out to make "red porcelain," probably because the formula seemed less elusive. He quickly mastered the production of a red stoneware that was harder than either Yixing or the Dutch copies, and which could be polished until the surface was as shiny as jasper, after which he named it. Serendipitously, kaolin clay was discovered at nearby Kolditz at about the same time, and by 1708, Böttger could claim to have found a workable mixture of kaolin and petuntse to produce the first true European hard-paste porcelain, creamy white and thinly potted, with only a slight green tinge to the foot rim. On January 24, 1710, the Meissen factory opened, to great fanfare.

We can only imagine the jig Augustus the Strong danced at the thought of all that porcelain he could now have made. His collection grew into what is now the Porzellansammlung, or "Johanneum Inventory," in Zwinger Palace, Dresden, Germany. (Web pages in English sometimes call the museum the Green Vault.) The collection of 20,000 objects miraculously survived Allied bombing in 1945, was seized and carried en masse to Russia by the retreating Red Army, and was returned only in 1958. Until the Berlin Wall came down, you had to cross into East Germany to view Augustus's collection of 80 17th- and 18th-century teapots. Now you may travel there unimpeded.

Eighteenth-century Meissen teapots are beautiful, expensive, and rare. Late-19th-century pots, however, can be found for $295.00–$650.00. In 1724 Meissen introduced the KPM (Königlich Porzellan Manufactur) mark; a year later, the factory started using the crossed-swords mark in underglaze blue (the mark is still used today) as well as gilt numbers added by the decorator. One particularly popular item was the Meissen Schneeballen tea service, produced during the 1740s. The ware is decorated with white flowers in relief and is unusual and interesting.

Meissen's secret recipe for porcelain did not stay secret for long; other European factories, some wooing away Meissen employees, sprang up in Vienna, Berlin, Venice,

Capodimonte (Italy), St. Cloud (France), and Vincennes (also France). Most produced soft-paste porcelain to start with, turning to hard-paste only when the technology, kaolin clay, and petuntse became available. A good example is the the Vincennes factory, which in 1759 moved to Sèvres, a village midway between Paris and Versailles, a convenient location for attracting royal patronage—in this case, that of Madame de Pompadour, mistress of King Louis XV of France. Kaolin clay was discovered in Limousin in 1768, and the first French hard-paste porcelain was made for presentation to Louis XV in December 1769. Both soft-paste and hard-paste were produced at Sèvres until 1804, when soft-paste was phased out.

Rule Britannia

Except for the Dutch, people who lived in Continental Europe during the 17th and 18th centuries took more to coffee and hot chocolate than to tea. According to Garth Clark, author of *The Eccentric Teapot*, while many of the new porcelain factories on the Continent produced tea services (in particular Meissen and Sèvres, whose enameled and gilded creations achieved heights of astonishing ostentation), "the exploration of teapot forms was never carried to the same level of obsession as it was in England. From 1750 onwards this small island dominated the art of creating teapots."

John Dwight of Fulham (now part of London) undoubtedly deserves the distinction of having made the first red stoneware teapot in England, about the same time Ary de Milde was turning them out in Holland. Red teapots were also made by two Dutch brothers, John-Philip and David Elers, who crossed to England during the last quarter of the 17th century and set up shop in Staffordshire. The Elers were so paranoid about their formulas being stolen that they refused to hire local potters. They also set up secretive, convoluted business practices; in the end when they were sued by Dwight for infringing his red-teapot patent, they couldn't absorb the cost and went bankrupt.

Today few examples of their teapots survive. W.B. Honey, author of *English Pottery and Porcelain*, believes that only four of the known pots usually claimed as the work of the Elers can be credited to them with any certainty. There are, however, a great many later versions of Elers-type teapots that some dealers like to call "Elers ware," even down to various Victorian redwares and modern Japanese Yixing-type pots. Buyer beware. On the other hand, who's to say that you won't find a real Elers teapot lurking on some junk-shop shelf, looking for all the world like a 19th-century Yixing or Japanese-Yixing knock-off? Keep your eyes peeled (the flip side of the buyer-beware coin).

The iron-rich clays of Staffordshire were perfect for making the much-clamored-for red teapots. Soon any number of potteries there were producing lead-glazed red earthenwares. English advances in clay refinement and molding techniques by the mid-18th century at long last enabled the production of excellent stoneware copies of Yixing teapots. Teapots from this time often are marked on the base with an unidentifiable pseudo-Chinese seal. Unfortunately, few of them have come down to us in one piece. According to Robin Hildyard of the Victoria and Albert Museum in London, writing in *The Story of the Red China Teapot*, which is posted at *www.thepotteries.org,* "although the 'Red China' itself was immensely strong, it was often used continuously almost to the point of destruction and then repaired with anything that would restore its original function: spouts, handles and lids of lead, tin, brass, silver or wood." People loved their red teapots to death, apparently—then fixed them with whatever came to hand. The English market was so glutted with red teapots by the 1770s, that Josiah Wedgwood despaired of getting any decent press whatsoever for his new Rosso Antico line.

Many Races of Teapots

The teapot business in England in the mid-18th century could barely keep up with demand and, in the phrase of John Bedford, author of *Talking about Teapots*, produced "many races" of teapots: There were red teapots; soft-paste porcelain "flying" teapots; stoneware teapots; slipware teapots; saltglaze teapots; black-glazed Jackfield-ware teapots; cream-colored teapots—a dizzying array considering that a mere century earlier there had been only Chinese porcelain and Yixing teapots. By the turn of the 18th century there were also silver pots, although few people could afford them. Queen Anne, who reigned from 1702 to 1714, gave her name to any number of lovely early-18th-century silver pots, the most popular of which may have been the pear-shaped, copied from a Yixing pot. Because silver conducts heat, pots made from it came to have wooden handles.

The bullet-shaped silver teapot became popular during the reign of King George I (1714–1727), superseding the pear-shape "in high fashion," according to Bedford, "and setting the pace for the endless porcelain and pottery styles" that followed. Somewhere around the year 1750, a Birmingham metalworker invented silver plating, fusing a thin coating of silver onto copper articles. Since the word *plate* was already used to refer to what we would now call sterling silver, the new silver-plated copper items came to be known as Sheffield plate. A fine Sheffield teapot, easily afforded by people for whom sterling silver teapots were out of reach, came to grace many a sideboard of the socially and economically ambitious. Britannia ware, a pewter-antimony alloy developed a few years later for those who could not afford even Sheffield, was also used to make teapots.

By the second quarter of the 18th century every pottery in England was turning out teapots. Scattered villages everywhere (but particularly in Staffordshire, where Burslem, Tunstall, Fenton, Longport, Cobridge, Hanley, Shelton, and Longton would later incorporate to form Stoke-on-Trent) produced many varieties of wares, including red teapots. But the more ambitious potteries wanted to produce something along the lines of porcelain from Jingdezhen. The opaque white of tin-glazed delftware offered wonderful decorative possibilities—like Chinese porcelain, you could paint it with bright colors (unlike the red pots, which were unamenable to color)— but delftware teapots, with their soft bodies and vulnerable glazes, were susceptible like the later soft-paste porcelain teapots to what Bedford bluntly called "sudden rape by boiling water"; most of them probably blew up.

What to do while waiting for English geniuses to duplicate the Meissen hard-paste formula? There was always saltglaze, or *saltzglatz*, as the Germans called it. Salt-

Rare Wedgwood-Whieldon teapot, ca. 1758 top left. Typical of Whieldon ware: cream-colored earthenware under a glaze showered with metallic oxides to give tortoiseshell or streaked effects. Photo courtesy Rufus Foshee.

Cauliflower teapot top right. Colored glazes, English, ca. 1760, of the type turned out by Whieldon-Wedgwood. Few 18th-century English teapots were marked. As John Bedford wrote in *Talking about Teapots*, "Whether a particular piece was made by [Wedgwood-Whieldon], or whether it was the work of admiring and envious neighbors, is, so far, anyone's guess." Photo courtesy Rufus Foshee.

glaze had been around for several hundred years, but someone got the idea to use it to make teapots. Salt thrown into the kiln during firing enhanced the hardness of the finished piece by vaporizing and glazing the pot. Early saltglaze teapots were dark in color, but eventually, by mixing different clays, grayish or off-whitish ware was achieved. These could be enjoyed in their pristine pale state like the Chinese *blanc de chine*, or decorated with colored lead glazes like delftware. Happily, saltglaze teapots were boiling-water resistant, and they refrained from flying. From about 1745, saltglaze wares could be cast in molds of plaster of Paris, freeing potters to create squirrel teapots, camel teapots, and house teapots, which because saltglaze presented such an ideal ground for painting, could be lavishly colored with bright enamels. Or, again, enjoyed white.

One innovation made by the famous Staffordshire potter Josiah Wedgwood (1730–1795) during his partnership with the nearly-as-famous Thomas Whieldon (1719–1795) in the late 1750s was the improvement of colored glazes, especially the intense green and yellow used on the "collyflower," pineapple, and cabbage teapots. Other potteries soon copied these designs and colors, but the Whieldon-Wedgwood pots were, in the words of Garth Clark writing in *The Eccentric Teapot*, "delicately walled, light as a feather, [and] perfectly balanced . . . a joy to behold."

**Polychrome
creamware
teapot, ca.
1770–1780.**
Photo courtesy
Rufus Foshee.

The Whieldon-Wedgwood partnership lasted only five years, as contracted, after which Wedgwood struck out on his own. Whieldon, among others, had made a cream-colored ware of Devonshire clay and flint (the same body that is used for saltglazed wares), usually with a hard alkaline or lead glaze, and Wedgwood began to tinker with the recipe. The result was a rich, buttery product, light and spare, and very fine in texture. Queen Charlotte, wife of King George III, liked it and ordered a service—at which point it became known as Queensware. Enormously popular, Queensware stayed in fashion until 1820. After the famous 1775 lawsuit settlement that allowed Staffordshire potters access to the kaolin clay deposits of Cornwall, heretofore reserved by patent to Richard Champion for Cookworthy's hard porcelain, Wedgwood was able to develop traditional creamware into a standardized product—moreover, one that could stand up to boiling water. Queensware teapots did not fly. Garth Clark is convinced that these industrial mass-production methods and Queensware's resilience together "encouraged the rapid spread of tea drinking in the West" perhaps more than any other product. There were "soon handsomely potted teapots and cups affordable to all but the very poor," he writes.

The Wedgwood factories, first at Ivy House, Burslem, Staffordshire, and subsequently at the Brick House Works, produced any number of wares in addition to the cauliflower, pineapple, and cabbage teapots and vaunted Queensware. A bisque (fired but not glazed) stoneware, called Jasper after the hard opaque quartz, was introduced in various colors about 1774. Most Wedgwood wares were made in the neoclassical designs in keeping with the classicism fad then rampant; the long-forgotten site of ancient Pompeii had been rediscovered in 1748 to great fanfare, and all things classic were romanticized in every kind of design, from furniture to architecture to teapots. Wedgwood still markets Jasper teapots today, in sage, primrose yellow, pink, Portland blue, and the registered-trademark Wedgwood blue.

"Old Wedgwood," produced before Josiah's death in 1795, is difficult to date. In 1860 the Wedgwood factory began marking wares with an impressed three-letter date code (see the Web site *www.thepotteries.org* for a chart to decode). Wares made after ca. 1770 were almost always impressed "WEDGWOOD," the exception being decorative pieces, which were marked "Wedgwood & Bentley" or "W. & B." from 1768 to 1780.

An innovation of the second half of the 18th century was transfer printing, a process by which paper transfers taken from copper plates were used to print engraved scenes onto ceramics. Classical scenes depicting Greek or Roman ruins, engraved portraits of famous men, and plates from books like *The Ladies Amusement* or *Liveres de Chinois* were all fair game for the black-printers, as the transfer printers were called. Most transfer work was not done at the potteries; rather, the plain wares were carted off to the black-printers, firms like Sadler & Green of Liverpool, which printed Wedgwood's wares for many years.

Lustre overglaze was a late-18th-century novelty that brought into being yet another race of teapots. First popularized by Islamic potters of the 9th century, this method of glazing, where gold, silver, and bronze could be added to the glaze, was refined in England by Josiah Wedgwood and Josiah Spode, producing an opalescent, iridescent finish. The trompe-l'oeil effect of these ceramic imitations of silver teapots was very realistic, and the pots became known as "poor man's Sheffield."

Another Wedgwood achievement was black basaltware teapots, named after the basaltic rock formations of the Giant's Causeway, in Northern Ireland. Unglazed, the pots were polished on a lapidary's wheel until they shone. Wedgwood himself noted that they were popular because they showed the whiteness of a lady's hand to perfection.

Blue Willow

Despite the craze for classicism at the end of the 18th century, there was still room in the hearts of English tea drinkers for romantic chinoiserie. The Willow pattern in the traditional blue underglaze is supposed to have originated around 1780 at the Caughley porcelain works in Shropshire, although this traditional attribution is legendary rather than factual. The pattern consists of a pastiche of teahouses, willow trees, footbridges, mandarins, fences, boats, lovers, rivers, and immortal doves, depicting the story of Koong-se, who falls in love with her father's secretary Chang and elopes with him. Chased by guards, the lovers escape in a boat to a distant land, where they build a simple life for themselves—except that Chang becomes a famous writer, which allows soldiers to track him down and kill him. Koong-se, deranged with grief, chooses suicide by fire, torching their house. Two doves show the lovers united in death.

So many variations of Blue Willow patterns have been since produced that it's impossible to trace them all, determine which is derivative of which, or take for granted that any given Blue Willow teapot is really as old as the person selling it says it is. Best not to buy unless the dealer is squeaky-clean reputable—or the price is low enough that you won't mind taking home a really nice fake. In the late 19th century, Worcester made a Willow-pattern double-spouted, single-chambered teapot with bail handle, among others. Twentieth-century versions of Blue Willow pattern teapots include Spode's Tower; and Booths Real Old Willow by Royal Doulton; there are countless others.

Unfortunately, I don't have room here to explore in detail all the many other different kinds of teapots made in England in the 18th century—Caneware, Prattware, the many diverse styles produced by the early soft-paste manufactories, to name only a few. Nor can I list all the individual potteries. Suffice it to say that the explosion in teapottery during that century was mind-boggling. For a thorough account, see John Bedford's book, *Talking about Teapots*, and Frank Tilley's *Teapots and Tea*.

Bone China, Eclecticism, Rockingham, and the Brown Betty

The first true English porcelain was manufactured by William Cookworthy in 1768. Unlike on the Continent, however, traditional kaolin-clay-petuntse porcelain was not destined to become the ware of choice in England. Many of the English soft-paste porcelain potters added animal-bone ash to their clay bodies, and early hard-paste manufacturers continued this practice; they simply added the bone ash to the kaolin-clay-petuntse formula. The result was bone china. Josiah Spode II is credited with inventing it in 1800.

The 19th century opened with an epoch of, in Garth Clark's words, "excessive, muddled eclecticism charac-terized by revivalist styles." A lot seemed to be going on. Napoleon was soon defeated, the Americans won the War of 1812, the British Industrial Revolution was well under way, and a little girl was born in 1818 who would come to the throne at age nineteen as Queen Victoria. Meanwhile, designs changed so quickly that a tea service two years old was considered scandalously passé, at least by the fervently fashionable. At the same time, retro was very much the thing: Louis XIV, Louis XV, rococo, baroque, and anything old that looked like it should be new again, mixed up and mashed together, with the re-sult, according to John Bedford, that "everything devel-oped a bulge and a fringe, rather like the hippopotami in Disney's *Fantasia* . . . But revival rococo gave us, bless it, the Rockingham teapot."

In the late 18th century, the Swinton Pottery, founded in 1745 on the Wentworth estate of the marquis of Rocking-ham in South Yorkshire, developed a distinctive rich-brown glaze containing manganese and iron. When brushed on and allowed to run, the glaze produced an attractive, streaky effect. Mary, the last marchioness of Rockingham (she died in 1804), liked teapots painted with this glaze, and over the course of her life ordered 230 of them, which may be how they came to the atten-tion of the Prince of Wales (later King George IV) when he visited Wentworth a few years after her death. He ordered a quantity of the small brown teapots and, following his example, so did the fervently fashionable. Perhaps it was then that the teapots, suddenly needing a name, came to be called Rockingham after their patroness, the dearly departed marchioness.

The original Rockingham pots had a tall, baluster shape and looked more like coffeepots, for which they are often mistaken—until one looks inside and sees the strainer at the base of the spout. Rockingham teapots certainly looked nothing like the later archetypal brown teapots considered their progeny, or the modern-day version, the Brown Betty. The terra-cotta-clay Brown Betty if anything is the rightful heir of the early 18th-century redware teapot; these pots are made in Stoke-on-Trent from clay which comes from the same area where the Elers brothers dug theirs in 1695. What the Rockingham teapot, the prototypical brown teapot, and the Brown Betty all do have in common is the Rockingham glaze, no longer streaky and now famous in its own right.

True Rockingham teapots are no longer made; the third Earl Fitzwilliam, tired of the mounting debts and questionable artistic judgment of the Brameld family managers, foreclosed the works in 1841. The glaze however was widely copied, both in England and America, and is now copied worldwide. Nineteenth-century American teapots made of medium to heavy pottery with a lustrous manganese brown glaze technically should be called American Rockingham, but the pottery is often called Bennington. The Bennington name also applies to modern, navy-blue spongeware handcrafted pottery, which has been made since 1948 by Bennington Potters and is itself widely copied. The confusion comes about because Bennington, Vermont, was the site of the Norton Pottery, established in 1785 and later called the United States Pottery Company, which produced yellowware glazed in the Rockingham style, afterwards copied by about 100 potteries in East Liverpool, Ohio; Pittsburgh; Baltimore; and elsewhere. Actual Bennington pots—made by Norton or the United States Pottery—command a much higher price than generic American Rockingham. Pieces made at Bennington from 1845–1847 were often marked "Norton and Fenton." Other marks include "Lyman Fenton & Co., Bennington, Vt." (1849–1850s) and the U.S.P.

Cadogan teapot. These lidless wonders were filled upside-down via a cork-stoppered hole in the bottom. They were originally copied from a kind of Chinese wine pot and allegedly brought to England by a Mrs. Cadogan. Made by the Rockingham factory as early as the 1830s, Cadogan pots were probably used to serve hot water, not tea.

ribbon mark from 1852–1858. Some pieces went unmarked, but are extremely difficult to authenticate.

One type of teapot drawn into the Rockingham-Bennington whirlpool is the Biblical-motif Rebekah-at-the-Well teapot, ca. 1850. Sometimes attributed to Derbyshire potter Edwin Bennett, who set up a pottery in East Liverpool, and elsewhere said to have been modeled by Charles Coxon for Bennett and Brothers of Baltimore, the design was copied at Bennington, although never with a true Rockingham glaze. Rebekah-at-the-Well became so popular it was thereafter copied everywhere else, even in Japan. Like the English redware teapots of the early 18th century, Rebekah teapots seem to have been loved to death; pots in pristine condition rarely come on the market, and according to Tina Carter will fetch $200.00 to $600.00.

A brief word about that odd bird, the Cadogan teapot. Modeled on a curious Chinese pot believed to have been originally designed for wine, the Cadogan pot has neither aperture nor lid and is filled through a small cork-stopped hole in the bottom. It would be very difficult to brew tea in one, because you'd never get the tea leaves out or be able to clean the thing. Yet these pots were produced by the Swinton Pottery of Rockingham fame, decorated in much the same way as the Rockingham pots, and sold as teapots by the hundreds. Some were painted

Caledonia Pottery

Presents

The Traditional Brown Betty Tea Pot Fully Hand Made at Old Caledonia Mills Stoke-on-Trent ENGLAND

Brown Betty. Manufactured from red clay for better heat retention and better-tasting tea, Brown Betty teapots are still made in Stoke-on-Trent, the same area where the Elers Brothers made their redware teapots in 1695. This one is from the Caledonia Pottery. Several sizes available at *www.britishtraditionals.com.*

with the words *hot water*, which gives a clue to their intended use. Tea in the 19th century was brewed to be extremely strong in a small teapot, and when served was diluted with hot water from a second pot. The Cadogan teapot, useless for any other tea-related purpose whatsoever, could at least be used to serve hot water. I tend to think that most of these pots, novelties that they were, wound up on a shelf for display purposes only.

No one knows how the Brown Betty teapot came to be so called, although one theory has it that the name was first used in the 1940s by American importers. Brown-glazed teapots, emblazoned with "For England and Democracy," packed with tea, and marked on the bottom "World War II, Escorted to U.S.A. by Royal Navy," were sent from England to the United States to aid the war effort. Perhaps these were the original Brown Bettys.

Personally, I like to imagine the gal the American importers had in mind was the valiantly cheerful, rosy-
cheeked Wren in her brown army uniform, giving her all
for Great Britain in its finest hour. But that's just me.

A Taste for Tea

The "excessive, muddled eclecticism" of British teapot
styles at the beginning of the 19th century was perhaps
due to the enormous increase in tea consumption at all
levels of society. During the 1700s, tea was so expensive
only wealthy British citizens could afford it; moreover it
was taxed at the astronomical rate of 119 percent. Despite
its prohibitive cost, the entire nation developed a taste for
tea, as did colonists in what would become the United
States. Servants dried and reused tea leaves from their
mistresses' tables. People who were not as wealthy
bought tea smuggled from Holland. Tea smuggling in
18th-century England was an enterprise about on par with
drug smuggling in 20th-century America, with the exception that very few people considered it an objectionable
practice. Parsons were even known to hide smuggled tea
in crypts beneath their churches. People justified the
smuggling by pointing at the unjustness of the tea tax.

The Americans showed their disdain for the tax by throw-
ing their tea into Boston Harbor in 1773. Richard Twining,
grandson of Thomas, with something of a vested interest, voiced his opposition to the tax by approaching
Prime Minister William Pitt the Younger for a word. Twining argued that by abating the tax, the government
would actually *increase* revenues because so many more
people would buy legally imported tea. Twining pre-
vailed, and the Commutation Act of 1784 reduced the tax
on tea. People bought the cheaper tea, the British government raked in as much tax as ever, and smuggling
ground to a halt overnight.

With the increase in tea consumption came an increase
in teapottery. Teapots became larger. Silver pots, earthenware, stoneware—all were made, used, and loved.
Simple bone-china tea sets were made for the mass
middle-class market, and opulent Regency bone-china tea
sets were produced for the nobility and upper classes,
particularly by Derby and Worcester. Staffordshire facto-

Old Oval–shaped teapot. Here shown in English Caneware, ca.1780. According to Miller's *Anthology,* "Spode's shape book of 1820 gives the name 'Old Oval' to the straight-sided, oval plan teapot, closely resembling a silver shape of the 1780s and 90s but produced in porcelain, and more rarely in earthenware." By the 1790s the Old Oval had superseded the round as the most popular teapot shape, but by the 1820s it was considered old-fashioned. It continued to be manufactured, however, to provide replacements. Photo courtesy Rufus Foshee.

ries like Davenport, Minton, Ridgway, and Spode prospered. Styles were copied, traded, lifted, stolen, and reproduced in different media. Silversmiths made silver pots in pottery shapes, potters made ceramic pots in silver shapes, the British copied Chinese styles, the Chinese copied British styles, and the Japanese made everything and anything, especially after Commander Perry's ships ended Japan's closure to the outside world in 1854. Dixons' 1840s Britannia metal teapots were widely imitated in silver by American firms like Reed and Barton of Taunton, Massachusetts, among others. The brave new world imported not only objects and ideas, but people, too. Potters from Staffordshire, transfer-printers from Liverpool, entrepreneurs, the industrial- and scientific-minded—workers from every potting walk of life—made their way to the United States of America, where good clay and plentiful supplies of coal awaited them. Potteries sprang up everywhere on both sides of the pond.

Staffordshire Blue

The most popular ware in the 1800s both in England and the United States was Staffordshire transfer-printed earthenware made by famous potters like Spode, Adams, Ridgway, Stevensons, and Clews. Teapots were decorated with the renowned Willow pattern, hunting and sporting tableaux, romantic and pastoral landscapes, entertaining anecdotal prints—anything and everything was fair game.

Blue
Staffordshire
teapot, ca.
1815–1820.
Photo courtesy
Rufus Foshee.

Most were underglaze blue, but many were made in pink, green, black, and other colors.

Thousands of shiploads of wares were exported from England to America, even with the success of nascent American potteries in Bennington, Vermont; Trenton, New Jersey; and East Liverpool, Ohio—as had been done even before the Revolutionary War. "Wedgwood literally dug himself into the trade by turning the first sod for the canal linking North Staffordshire to the port of Liverpool," writes John Bedford. "Hardly was the [Revolution] over than he was busy selling to the Americans medallions of Washington and Franklin." After the War of 1812, exports of British teapots and other wares to America resumed—many printed with scenes celebrating the American victory, or American landscapes. Staffordshire in fact dispatched painters and engravers to sketch American themes. Many a mid-19th-century "American" teapot on closer inspection turns out to be English-made.

Lustreware teapots were also popular. Their metallic glazes gave the effect of silver, gold, or copper, and the pots were also made in pink or purple tones. Sunderland was a pink lustre with a mottled or marbled effect.

The so-called "barge" teapot was made in both gallon and half-gallon size, and it became a must-have for any fashionable garden party. Its salient features are a teapot-shaped finial and an inscription plate upon which could be printed or inscribed any sort of sentiment, epitaph, personal message, birth announcement, or inane ditty. "Tis Very Rare to Have Such a Lot So Have a Drink from Our Teapot," proclaimed one barge teapot made near Barton-on-Trent about the time of Queen Victoria's Diamond Jubilee. Barge teapots are really a sub-genre of folk art; their tradition arose among people who lived on the canals (hence the name), and most were made in tiny one-person potteries that for the most part declined and disappeared one by one after World War I. Modern-day potter Joanne DeLomba has produced a whimsical and imaginative modern version; she calls it a "Tea Cup Teapot," referring to its antecedents only as "a whimsical folk art style." DeLomba's pot is unmistakably a barge: 11.5 inches tall, capable of brewing a full 10 cups, with a teapot-shaped finial.

In the 1840s Toby-With-a-Wooden-Leg teapots became popular: a piratic-looking Toby of jug fame sits with his legs splayed up, the "wooden" leg forming the spout and the "good" leg the handle. Of the same ilk, teapots with the faces of Dickens characters flooded the market at the height of that writer's popularity. A teapot in the form of the three-legged symbol of the Isle of Man became so sought-after, it was made for years and years and years from the same molds; for this reason, these pots are difficult to date. And where would the Victorian teapot be without its flowers? Wordsworth's primrose was only one of the many blossoms to burst into bloom on 19th-century pots.

The Duchess of Bedford, Earl Grey, and Assam Tea

Almost as soon as tea arrived in England, the very British tea ceremony was born: unlocking the tea caddy, brewing the tea, serving the guests each with a cup, saucer, and spoon, offering milk and sugar, replenishing each cup when it was set down upon the table. All this was carried out with grace, elegance, and fanfare by the mistress of the tea table. There were stories of hapless Frenchmen who, ignorant of the custom of placing one's spoon in one's cup to signal "no more, please," found themselves downing ten or twelve cups until, with bursting bladders, they fled the room. Implied is that their predicament was their own fault for being ignorant. Anyone who was anyone knew the ritual.

Anna Maria Stanhope (1783–1857), duchess of Bedford, is credited with inventing the tea ceremony to end all tea ceremonies, that pleasant repast known as Afternoon Tea. Legend has it that one afternoon Her Grace, complaining of a "sinking feeling," sent for a pot of tea and a "few nice delicate things to eat," in the words of Sam Twining. Whether this was before or after the duchess was appointed Lady of the Bedchamber to the young Queen Victoria when she came to the throne in 1837 is uncertain, but lovers of tea lore like to imagine that Her Grace one day put a word into the ear of the queen. In any case, the British have been enjoying afternoon tea with little sandwiches and pastries ever since.

One great contribution to tea drinkers everywhere was that of Charles, second earl Grey (1764–1845), prime minister under King William IV, who gave his name to what is today the most popular specialty tea. Legend has it that His Lordship sent an envoy on a diplomatic mission to China, where the envoy allegedly saved the life of a Mandarin. The grateful Mandarin sent the earl an appreciative gift of exotically scented tea. His Lordship asked Twinings to duplicate it. Today there are many versions of Earl Grey tea on the market, generally a blend of large-leaf Chinese tea, Darjeeling, and oil of Bergamot (a Mediterranean citrus), but Twinings lays claim to the recipe closest to the original Mandarin's gift.

One more important item of 19th-century tea history took place in Assam. Despite the Opium Wars Great Britain waged with China from 1839 to 1842, the prize of which was the opening of various Chinese ports to foreign trade and the ceding of Hong Kong, what the British really wanted was to grow their own tea. All kinds of industrial espionage took place, including stolen tea bushes smuggled into junks during the dead of night, but what finally solved the problem was the discovery in Assam, India, of tea bushes growing wild. India was then part of the British Empire. The tea was cultivated in Assam with varying rates of success, then transplanted to Ceylon (now Sri Lanka). Assam tea was first sold at London auction in 1839. As Sam Twining tells it, "This tea was stronger, more pungent, and maltier than any previous tea from China; anyone who did not take milk

already would have done so now." Assam tea had an added benefit: because it was from a British colony, this tea had no duty imposed on it. By the end of the century, sales of Indian tea would surpass those of Chinese tea. Cheaper tea meant more tea drinkers than ever before—and more teapots.

Minton Majolica

Minton, founded in the 1790s, in all likelihood started out with underglaze blue transferware teapots then in fashion, although none so far have come down to us. The first teapots to carry a Minton mark, according to Paul Atterbury and Maureen Batkin, editors of *The Dictionary of Minton*, were those made in the bone-china tableware range, ca. 1800–1816. By 1850, Minton teapots were being produced in every material in use at the factory, in styles and patterns to suit all levels of the market; the range also included toy teapots, which were made in three sizes in 1842.

The perennial Minton favorites are the majolica teapots. The Minton majolica glaze was introduced to the public at the Great Exhibition of All Nations in 1851 at the Crystal Palace in London, where it was awarded a prize for "beauty and originality of design." The teapots were made from the 1860s in at least twelve designs, including vegetables, a cockerel, a fish swallowing a fish, the famous vulture and python, the equally famous Magot or dwarf holding a Noh mask, and—perhaps the most famous—a monkey entwined around a fruit. Several of

Aesthetic Teapot, Royal Worcester Porcelain Company. First produced in 1880 as a spoof on Oscar Wilde and the Aesthetes, proponents of anti-industrial, art-for-art's-sake school. Made of eggshell-thin porcelain; surviving examples are extremely rare.

these teapots were reintroduced in the early 1930s, and again in the 1990s. The 1990s pots are clearly marked with a special Minton Archives backstamp. An original Vulture & Python teapot sold at Christie's in 2001 for £46,875.00 ($75,242.50 at conversion rates at this writing); a Minton Archives Vulture & Python copy is currently available at the Royal Doulton Web site for £495.00 ($794.56).

The Aesthetic Teapot

Perhaps the most famous 19th-century teapot of all time is the Aesthetic Teapot by Royal Worcester Porcelain Company. This rare gem—actually rare gems, as the pot was produced in two similar but not exactly alike forms— was first made in 1880 as a spoof on Oscar Wilde and the Aesthetes, proponents of an anti-industrial, art-for-art's-sake school that later evolved into the Arts and Crafts Movement.

In 1875 Wilde, then a student at Oxford University, came into possession of two blue and white vases, about which he quipped, "I find it harder and harder every day to live up to my blue china." While it's hard for us to understand from our standpoint exactly why, the remark at the time caused nearly the same furor as John Lennon's 1960s comment that the Beatles were more popular than Jesus. Clerics sermonized against "heathenism," moralists raged, and the very honor of red-blooded Englishmen was impugned. Wilde was catapulted to notoriety. Punch cartoons and George Du Maurier caricatures, in one of which a young matron fervently vowed to live up to her new Japanese teapot, fanned the flames into a national bonfire.

When the teapot was unveiled, it seemed to capture the moment. In the form of a languid, limp-wristed man with a sunflower on one side and a languid, limp-wristed woman with a lily on the other, the pot was inscribed on the base with the words, "The fearful consequences through the laws of Natural Selection and Evolution of living up to one's teapot." The teapot thus in David Battie's words managed

". . . in one brilliant flash of humour to poke fun at the Aesthetes (the limp wrist and bisexual lid); Oscar Wilde (the lily and the sunflower); the Gosvenor Gallery (which held an exhibition of one blue and white teapot); Darwin (whose evolutionary theories were still under debate) and Gilbert and Sullivan (the greenery-yallery clothes)."

Battie concluded, "No other ceramic work of art of any period comes close to encapsulating the period in which it was made so effectively." The pot itself was produced in eggshell-thin porcelain, "making its survival in good shape highly unlikely." Indeed, most broke; those that have come down to us have chips or restoration. Battie's estimated price for one in 1994: £1,800.00–£2,500.00 ($2,889.29–$4,012.90 at conversion rates at this writing).

Simple Yet Perfect

Every collector of teapots who drinks tea sooner or later wrestles with the question of how to prevent stewing. When you leave tea leaves in a teapot past their optimal brewing time, they stew, releasing tannic acid and turning the infusion bitter. Nowadays we're used to simple solutions like teaballs and infusion baskets that allow us to remove the leaves from the tea when it's finished brewing. But Victorians liked gadgets. While I don't have room here to go into all the various English and American inset-infuser teapots patented between 1817 and 1912, one that deserves mention is the S.Y.P.—the Simple Yet Perfect tip-over teapot invented by the earl of

Dundonald in 1901, with an improved version in 1905. The twelfth earl, a career military man, designed the pot to tip over and lie on its back for brewing, then stand upright again—retaining the leaves in the top compartment, separate from the infusion.

Several potteries, including Wedgwood, intrigued by the design, turned out S.Y.P. teapots. There was even a silver version. As a novelty the pots sold briskly, but they never outpaced the traditional teapot. Renamed the Ceylon Teapot, the S.Y.P. had a short career in America in advertisements and promotions for Ceylon tea.

Art Deco and the Racing Car Teapot

The art nouveau movement spanned the change in century and was popular up until World War I, but its effect on teapottery was negligible. In the 1920s and 1930s, on the other hand, what we now call art deco was very well represented in ceramics. They style was variously called Industrial Moderne, Jazz Moderne, and Streamline Moderne, and the name *art deco* didn't come into play until the 1960s, by which time the style itself was passé. Decorators looking back with the benefit of hindsight pinned the look to the Exposition Internationale des Arts Décoratifs et Industriels Modernes, which was held in Paris in 1925. The show displayed a pastiche of styles: Tutankhamen's Egypt, pre-Columbian Mexico, Greek Mythology, Cubism, Futurism, and Constructivism.

"Art Deco had no weighty aspirations," Alan Riding wrote recently in the *New York Times* in an article about a current show at the Victoria and Albert Museum in London. "It aimed to be glamorous, entertaining, sexy, exotic and outrageous. As Europe slid toward disaster, it offered escapism."

Clarice Cliff's brightly colored, geometric designs certainly fit the art deco bill; her Bizarre Ware teapots, jugs, and other pieces made her a household name in the 1930s. Her Indian Teepee Teapot currently sells for about $1,375.00; a more conventional, utilitarian teapot of her design from the same time period recently sold for £335.00 ($536.59 at conversion rates at this writing).

Perhaps the most famous art deco teapot is the original Sadler pre-1947 racing car teapot with the license plate reading OKT42 (Okay tea for two). First made in 1937, the pot is now a collector's item. The early teapots came in several colors finished in a platinum lustre, which looks like chrome plate. A pre–World War II teapot will be marked on the bottom with "Made in England" and with the design registration number 820236. In 1939, Sadler, like most British industries, stopped producing ceramics and turned its business to the war effort; the OKT42 teapot production ceased until 1945. After the war, silver (used to make platinum lustre) was in short supply. Sadler instead glazed the teapots in one color, then applied a slightly different color with a sponge. The OKT42 number plate was no longer applied. Even cheaper to produce than the two-tone teapots were teapots in a single color.

A small number of post-war teapots were, however, finished with the expensive platinum lustre; these are recognizable by their Sadler backstamp, and, very often, the decorator's initials. They are worth a great deal more than the single-color car teapots.

Some cream-colored car teapots were decorated with Mabel Lucy Atwell transfers and an orange glaze instead of the platinum lustre. The *Guardian* (London) recently estimated that Mabel Lucy Atwell car teapots would cost £600.00–£700.00 ($963.11–$1,123.63 at conversion rates at this writing), whereas a single-color yellow or green car teapot would fetch only £100.00–£120.00 ($160.52–$321.04).

Production of the racing car teapot ceased in 1952 when the factory, like most of the decorative industries in Great Britain, turned its attention to making commemorative pieces for the coronation of Queen Elizabeth II. The original molds, however, were later acquired by Peter Wood, a passionate collector of art deco novelty teapots. Wood still had them a few years ago when a fellow collector called, distraught over having broken the lid on his OKT42 teapot. Wood suggested casting a new one. Word got around; Wood was soon besieged with requests, and Racing Teapots was formed around some of the finest potters and decorators in Stoke-on-Trent.

Today Racing Teapots Ltd. produces not only reproductions of the original OKT42 car teapots, but also repro-

Queen Mary Ocean Liner teapot. Modern reproduction made by Racing Teapots Ltd. from the same mold for the 1936 original. Available at this writing for $98.00 at *www.abitofbritain.com.*

ductions made from other molds Peter Wood bought at the same time he acquired the car teapot molds: the ocean liner teapot, which can be painted as several different ships, including the *Queen Mary, Mauritania,* and *Titanic;* the aeroship teapot; and the tank teapot with a Winston Churchill look-alike driver peering out the turret. At this writing, these reproductions are available for $98.00 each at *www.abitofbritain.com.*

The teapots actually on the *Queen Mary* and other great ocean liners of the period, as well as on the great transcontinental railroads, would not have been ship or train teapots but rather cube teapots, designed to stack well in cramped galleys rather than to pour well. Reportedly, cube teapots leaked and dripped their way across land and sea, often paired with matching cube milk pitchers and cube sugar bowls on little trays. Whether the stability afforded by the square shape offset the drippiness is the question. But they were popular then and have since become popular with collectors. In good condition a plain cube teapot runs about £30.00–£40.00 ($48.16–$64.21 at conversion rates at this writing); a desirable pattern may spike the price to £200.00 ($320.36); and a silver-plated pot to as much as £500.00 ($862.59).

Art deco essentially waned as the looming World War II waxed. Like Sadler, producers of the cube teapot in Great Britain were caught in the maw of the war effort. At war's end, no one wanted to look back, and teapot buyers like everyone else fixed their gaze on the future.

Tank teapot. Modern reproduction made by Racing Teapots Ltd. from the same mold for the 1938 original. This teapot was first made in the 1920s with a driver modeled on "Old Bill," a cartoon character popular during World War I; by 1938 the mold had been altered so the driver resembled Winston Churchill. Available at this writing for $98.00 at *www.abitofbritain.com.*

Commemorative Teapots

The big event in Great Britain in the early 1950s was the coronation of Queen Elizabeth II. As the British had looked to their new queen's parents to guide them through the war, they now looked to the 25-year-old Elizabeth to lead them to restored prosperity.

Queen Elizabeth I was probably the first English monarch to have her image painted on a plate, but since she lived in the days when people still drank ale for breakfast, hers was not the first to grace a teapot. That honor seems to have gone to William III and Mary II, who came to the throne in 1685 after James II was packed off to France. Images of these monarchs were painted on a teapot decorated in Holland. Thereafter the royal family may very well have rued the day their images appeared on anything other than coinage. It wasn't long before the average Staffordshire potter realized the market potential of commemorating the comings and goings of the royals on jugs, tankards, plates, and teapots. Hardly had the nascent English teapot business established itself in the early 18th century than potters began cranking out pots to commemorate any occasion: According to David Battie, "The Retreat of Napoleon, the (temporary) Recovery of King George III from madness, the disgraceful affair of the Duke of York, the death of Princess Charlotte; all took place in the first twenty years of the 19th century and all survive in ceramic form."

Prices for royal commemoratives are oddly unpredictable and depend on factors I have not yet been able to determine. The Wedgwood items always seem to go for more; the common crockery rarely appreciates unless you hold onto it for, say, a hundred years or so. King Edward VIII, who abdicated for the woman he loved to become the duke of Windsor, usually brings a pretty penny in porcelain or bone china, but not in common crockery. Prices of Princess Diana commemoratives shot through the roof shortly after her death; they've come down quite a bit since then. An aluminum teapot commemorating the silver jubilee of King George V and Queen Mary, with a dark wood handle, recently went for as little as $65.00, even though many of its brother and sister teapots were undoubtedly turned in during the World War II metal drives. A King George VI and Queen Elizabeth 1937 chromium-plated coronation teapot recently sold for only $26.00. On the other hand, a VE Day commemorative ceramic teapot sold for £160 ($256.83 at conversion rates at this writing) in 2001. My advice? If you're going to collect commemorative teapots, go for high-end bone china or porcelain; these will more likely be something worth leaving your grandchildren.

Miniature and Toy Teapots

It might seem that people who collect teapots and people who collect *miniature* teapots are one and the same breed, but collectors of miniature teapots might beg to differ—seemingly, never the twain shall meet. Toy teapots, which are not the same as miniature, are a subspecialty altogether. Edward Bramah recommends two books: *Understanding Miniature British Pottery and Porcelain 1730–Present Day*, by Maurice and Evelyn Milbourn, and *English Toy China*, by Doris Anderson Lechler.

Miniature teapots have been made since the 18th century. For the most part they have been produced as part of complete tiny tea and dinner services, and many were made by famous potteries such as Bow, Limoge, Spode, Minton, Wedgwood, and Worcester in the same shapes and patterns as the full-size sets; many of these firms continue to produce miniature teapots and tea services today. There are Blue Willow miniatures, Wedgwood jasperware miniatures, underglaze blue and white designs—in short, all pots Lilliputian. There are even tiny Limoge *veilleuse-théières,* and minuscule brass teapots from India.

Miniature teapots have enjoyed a resurgence in popularity since World War II, but especially since the 1970s. Recently they have begun to be sold in sets of teapots, as opposed to sets of dishes; for example, ten miniature Yixing teapots offered together. Miniature teapots are also now sold individually, usually from between $10.00 and $25.00. Antiques are, of course, more expensive. At the 2001 Law Fine Art sale of the Joseph Jackson Collection, believed to be the largest sale of small teapots ever held, a Masons Ironstone miniature teapot, ca. 1815–1820, went for £780.00 ($1,249.41 at conversion rates at this writing), and a Spode miniature teapot ca. 1820 sold for £620.00 ($993.12). The problem for the average collector may be the unscrupulous dealer attempting to pass off modern reproductions of tiny teapots as bonafide antiques. Tina Carter cites as an example "new floral teapots made in Japan, about two inches high, which have a pattern similar to those made in the 1940s and 1950s. Most Japanese teapots of that era were marked with red or black backstamps; those with no mark or a gold paper label may be modern." Since paper labels are most often removed, the only indication of age may be a bisque, unglazed bottom. Occasionally older Japanese miniatures show an unglazed or bisque interior as well.

Cardew tiny teapots have recently found a place in collectors' hearts. Each year Cardew produces a handful of new designs whose quality and detail rivals that of their full-size companions; the current crop can be ordered individually, or as a set of ten together with a teapot-shaped display shelf for $120.00. The Cardew Web site is *www.teapotdepot.com.*

Miniature teapots are so lightweight it's a good idea to secure them to their display shelf. Tina Carter recommends tiny dabs of Quake Hold or some other sticky material.

There is one caveat in the buyer-beware category: often teapots are advertised as miniatures when what the seller really means is individual serving–size, for example a so-called "miniature" teapot on one Web site that

Big Ben figural teapot. Marked on bottom, "Hand painted Price Kensington Potteries, Made in England." Available at this writing from Portobello China and Woollens Ltd., London. Purchased in 2003 and probably made that year.

"holds 2 cups = 16 oz." Some Yixing teapots may brew only two ounces of tea; these too may be advertised as miniatures. They may or may not fit your personal ideal of what is miniature and what is not.

Figural Teapots

As we have already seen in Chapter 1, teapots in the shape of animals, persons, houses, vegetables, fruits, automobiles, birthday cakes, pianos—in short, virtually in the shape of anything—are not new. Ancient Chinese teapots came in some of these shapes (perhaps with the exception of automobiles, birthday cakes, and pianos), and modern teapots have come in all shapes ever since.

The collector who is interested in figural teapots usually is specifically interested in one type: house teapots, say, or elephant teapots. Watching the eBay listings can be helpful here; and a Google search of Web sites from time to time may net results. Use simple search terms in quotations marks—"house teapot," "elephant teapot," for example—and be prepared for the odd result: A search for "house teapot" will also produce Web sites of suppliers with *house* in their names, and teapots decorated with house patterns. Skip these sites. So far I have not run across any physical, brick-and-mortar shop that sells only house teapots or elephant teapots—although one may exist unbeknownst to me. (If you know of one, let me know.)

The houses, or English cottage teapots, have been so popular over the years that you could build a borough larger than Manhattan with them. They are not particularly well-designed for brewing tea, as most of them are square, although many undoubtedly produce the morning cuppa for their owners as dutifully as any Brown Betty. There have been Yixing house teapots since the dawn of teapottery, and it is not difficult to find modern versions of the old designs or reproductions. Saltglaze house teapots from 18th-century Staffordshire often depicted the Big House in Burslem, home of the Wedgwood family; nowadays house teapots come in the shape of any house imaginable, encompassing the most expansive definition of the concept: cottages, churches, castles, inns, government buildings, national monuments, synagogues, or even mosques, and are often made as souvenirs of major tourist sites, including Big Ben, Harrods, and St. Paul's Cathedral.

The most popular design may be the house with the thatched roof. Edward Bramah, musing on the attraction of these country cottage teapots, says, "Perhaps they represent an ideal and carefree country life, sitting on the kitchen shelf, which is pleasant to be reminded of even though it may be unattainable and less than ideal when attained." James Sadler and Sons, Ltd., originally founded in Burslem in the late 1800s, produced any

Andy Titcomb elephant teapot. Seems to have more of that elusive *je-ne-sais-quoi* elephant-ness than other elephant teapots. Available at this writing for $58.00 at *www.abitofbritain.com.*

number of house teapots in the century following, including the Country Crafts series and English Country Houses series. (They also produced the famous cat teapots; see below.) Unfortunately, as the new millennium dawned, Sadler was taken over by Churchill China.

One figural-teapot name to conjure with is Paul Cardew, who makes dozens of delightful pots, including all sorts of houses, furniture, Disney characters, Winnie the Pooh, and others; see the Cardew Web site, *www.teapotdepot.com*.

I would be remiss if I did not mention cat teapots. These are usually in the form of a seated cat with one paw outstretched to form the spout. The cat's tail curves up onto the cat's back to form the handle. If you are a cat teapot lover, I doubt you need me to tell you where to buy cat teapots. Personally, I prefer dragon teapots to cat teapots. Luckily there are thousands of figural teapots to suit any figural-teapot taste imaginable, however, so you don't have to listen to me.

America the Beautiful

Potters were among the earliest immigrants to the British Colonies that would later become the United States. Some were potting around on this side of the pond as early as early as 1635. But there was no way they could compete with either Chinese export porcelain transshipped from England or the growing pottery industry in Great Britain. There was also a conspiracy by the Brits to suppress all colonial manufactures, in order to keep America tied to her mother's apron strings.

This changed of course with the American Revolution, first because people boycotted British goods, then because there weren't any British goods arriving because of the war. Earthenware and stoneware operations had to increase production to fill the gap in supply. A few years later, the War of 1812 caused the same problem. But when there was no war, Americans liked Chinese export porcelain and Staffordshire wares more than they liked what their own potters could turn out. It wasn't until the mid-19th century that the American potting industry really got off the ground.

Twinspout Teamaster, ca. 1940. Marked on the bottom, "Twinspout Teamaster, Patent 2135410, made in U.S.A." Made by Hall and marketed by the Twinspout Pottery Company, this pot has two chambers, one with a strainer at the base of the spout and one without, for tea and hot water respectively. A pot like this recently sold for $95.00. Teapot courtesy Miriam Novalle, T Salon & T Emporium.

Individual small potters had of course thrived in their own communities, including the Norton Pottery in Bennington, Vermont. There was certainly enough clay. The main source for many years for many potteries up and down the East Coast was the rich deposit of fine blue clay centered at South Amboy, New Jersey, and extending to Staten Island and Long Island, New York. Kaolin had been dug as early as 1738 in Virginia. As settlers moved west, the Ohio River Valley opened up. Trenton, New Jersey, became known as "the Staffordshire of America," while East Liverpool, Ohio, became "America's Crockery City."

It wasn't until 1918 that the White House ordered its official state service from an American company. That company was Lenox, and it remains the only American china in continuous use at the White House. According to Lenox, "about half of all fine porcelain dinnerware purchased since the 1950s in this country bears the Lenox backstamp." That may be true. Personally, I think about half the teapots collected since the 1950s in this country were made by Hall China in East Liverpool, Ohio.

Founded in 1903, Hall recently celebrated its 100th anniversary with a special edition anniversary teapot in several colors. There is a Hall Collectors Club you should contact if you're thinking of collecting Hall teapots; they have a Web site whose address is

Skytone teapot by Homer Laughlin, ca. 1950s. Marked on the bottom, "Skytone by Homer Laughlin, U.S.A., K56N8." The blue color of the body is not a glaze application but rather the color of the clay; the glaze is clear. White clay used for the handles and finials gives the line it's signature two-tone look. Teapot courtesy Miriam Novalle, T Salon & T Emporium.

www.inter-services.com/HallChina/. There are actually several Hall Clubs; check them out. A Google search on the terms "Hall," "china," and "collectors" should yield several. Another notable club is at *www.chinaspecialties.com*.

Hall is primarily in the business of restaurant and hotel ware, billing their goods as "the densest, hardest porcelain bodies of all other china cookingware," in particular their freezer-to-oven-to-tableware. The company's fun collectibles are from the 1920s and 1930s on. During the art deco era Hall produced cube teapots, among others. One cube set included two pots, one for tea and one for hot water, snuggled together onto a recessed tray; this twin set was used at Rumplemeyers for many years and now sells for about $75.00. In the 1920s Hall came out with its Gold Decorated line, adding gold trim to three of its solid-colored restaurant teapots; housewives snapped them up, delighted with their durability.

Another enormously popular Hall venture was the Autumn Leaf line, first produced for the Jewel Tea Company in 1933 as a give-away premium. Discontinued two years later, the teapot was later resurrected by China Specialties as a commissioned reissue. Hall also produced premiums for McCormick Tea and Lipton, among others. For this reason many Hall teapots are not marked "Hall" but rather bear the names of the companies for whom the

promotions were made. Some promotional pots will carry Hall's motto, "Superior Quality," which may be used to identify a Hall teapot even if it's not marked "Hall."

Another American pottery worth mentioning is the Homer Laughlin China Company, originally of East Liverpool but since the turn of the 20th century of Newell, West Virginia, across the Ohio River. It was at Homer Laughlin that Frederick Hurton Rhead designed Fiesta ware, which was first introduced in 1936. Fiesta was discontinued in 1973, but reintroduced in in 1986 and is still made today. The Fiesta teapot was an icon of the 1950s, appearing in the background of many of the *Leave It to Beaver*-type kitchens so popular with advertising executives then. An old Fiestaware teapot from the 1950s can be had these days for about $299.00; or you can buy a new one for $24.95. The old one will be semi-vitrified earthenware; the new one high-fired, fully vitrified china.

There are more American potteries than can be encompassed within the scope of a book like this. Many factories produced a standardized product; others were craft potteries turning out handcrafted, hand-painted pieces. One worth mentioning is the Biloxi Art and Novelty Pottery, which was created in 1890 by George Ohr. This eccentric character with his long droopy mustache turned out such wonderful teapots, one sold this year for $55,812.50. Imagine going on the *Antiques Roadshow* with *that*.

Kettle teapot by Ian Rylatt. Ceramic pot with metallic-looking glaze, 10 in. high. Available at this writing for $120.00 at *www. abitofbritain.com.*

Novelty Teapots

The Arts and Crafts Movement of the late 19th century was a swing in the opposite direction of industrialization and the effects of industrialization on the decorative arts. In England, craft potters (also called studio potters) decamped from Staffordshire and other large potteries for the relative obscurity of Somewhere Else, where they molded wares by hand, decorated them by hand, operated the kilns themselves, and then sold the wares. World War I is usually considered the end of the Arts and Crafts Movement. But its spirit never fully died, and it's not hard to imagine that spirit, like the genie in Aladdin's lamp, curling languidly out of modern craft teapots today.

As noted in Chapter 1, many modern craft teapots, often called "novelties," are not designed to brew tea. As galley owner Garth Clark, author of *The Eccentric Teapot*, puts it, "Often it is the tension between these wildly improbable forms and the traditional function of the teapot that

inspires the humor, irony, and strange genius of the truly peculiar teapot." The teapot serves no longer as a vessel for tea but as "a container of unusual ideas, a familiar format for expressing the unfamiliar." The chickenwire teapot of Leopold Foulem might best express this concept; it could hardly contain a liquid, let alone anything else more material than an idea.

That said, many craft potters today do make pots you can brew tea in. They may not brew as well as a Brown Betty, and some may present a challenge to clean, but they're "real" teapots in the traditional sense. One particularly lovely teapot with traditional, functional lines is Angela Glover's Mice and Corn teapot. While not hand-thrown, Glover's unique designs are conceived, hand drawn, and individually painted and signed by the artist at her Artfire Pottery, near Lairg, Sutherland, Scotland.

Ian Rylatt, working in North Bennington, England, makes ceramic teapots that when glazed look like metal.

Not all craft potters live and work far from the maddening crowd; at Bairstow Manor Pottery in Stoke-on-Trent, a third generation of Bairstow family potters produces whimsical Carlton Ware teapots, among them Elvis-in-Plane and Churchill-in-Plane teapots in limited editions of 1,000. These are available at *www.abitofbritain.com* for $135.00 each. Swineside Teapottery, Tony Carter's Teapot Pottery, and Cardew all make teapots cast and decorated by hand. The list of craft potters working today seems endless—all the better for us teapot collectors.

Ms. At'teatude by Gary Seymour. Modern young woman, complete with designer jewelry, cell phone in hand, and a look-but-don't-touch stance. 28 cm. high, 20 cm. wide. Available at this writing for $120.00 at *www. abitofbritain.com.*

Royal Doulton English cottage teapot. Teapot courtesy Miriam Novalle, T Salon & T Emporium.

Carltonware Elvis in a Plane. Limited edition of 1,000. Available at this writing for $135.00 at *www. abitofbritain.com.*

Garth Clark really deserves the final word when it comes to novelty teapots. His books, *The Artful Teapot* and *The Eccentric Teapot*, are delights with which to while away a pleasant afternoon or evening, a pot of tea at hand, perhaps even a plate of cucumber sandwiches. So what if many of the teapots in his books couldn't brew tea even if they wanted to? Who, after all, says we can own only one teapot? Why not at least two, the Brown Betty for tea, and the sculptural, nonfunctional novelty for eye candy? Why not three? Or more?

Perhaps now might be a good time to quote Juliet, rhapsodizing about Romeo: "My bounty is as boundless as the sea."

No reason the same thing can't be said about one's teapots. ◾

RESOURCE GUIDE

ANTIQUES SHOPS OF NOTE

Asia House
Les Solomon
P.O. Box 6002
Lancaster, PA 17607-6002
tel.: 717-397-6435
Web site: www.trocadero.com/solo36/

Fine Chinese export porcelain, including teapots.

Hanes & Ruskin Antiques
111 Boston Post Road
Old Lyme, CT 06371
tel.: 860-434-1800
Web site: www.hanesandruskin.com

Eighteenth- and early-19th-century American high-style country furniture and accessories, including teapots.

Julie Lindberg Antiques
P.O. Box 89
Wayne, PA 19087-0089
tel.: 610-697-5906, 1-800-768-2647
Web site: www.julielindbergantiques.com

Fine Americana—Canton, including teapots.

Maria and Peter Warren Antiques, Inc.
Antiques and Decorative Arts
1030 Ridgefield Road
Wilton, CT 06897
tel.: 203-762-7353
E-mail: warren.antiques@snet.net

Early creamware, pearlware, and other fine ceramics, including teapots.

William R. & Teresa F. Kurau
Historical Staffordshire and Collector's Items
P.O. Box 457
Lampeter, PA 17537
tel.: 717-464-0590

Historical Staffordshire, including teapots.

APPRAISERS

Appraisers Association of America
386 Park Avenue South
Suite 2000
New York, NY 10016-8804
tel.: 212-889-5404

The oldest nonprofit association of personal property appraisers, with approximately 1,000 members in more than 600 subspecialties in all areas of fine art, antiques, and insurance appraisals.

BOOKS, MAGAZINES, AND NEWSLETTERS

See the Bibliography for recommended books. Most books listed are available at this writing through *www.abebooks.com*; otherwise, any bookstore can order whatever you want. (Personal plug: patronize independent booksellers whenever possible.) Copies of most books in the Bibliography can also be found in the New York Public Library, General Research Division (Main Branch). Not near New York City? Your local librarian will surprise you with what he or she can obtain on interlibrary loan; give it a whirl.

Shire Books produces small books on topics such as Spode, Copeland, Minton, and other pottery and porcelain manufacturers. You can cruise their inventory online or request a free catalog.

Shire Publications Ltd.
Cromwell House
Church Street
Princes Risborough
Buckinghamshire HP27 9AA
England
tel.: 44-1844-344301
E-mail: shire@shirebooks.co.uk

TEA: A Magazine
P.O. Box 348
Scotland, CT 06264
tel.: 888-456-8651
Web site: www.teamag.com

Tea, tearooms, teapots, and all things tea related. At the Web site, you can click on each back issue and see the table of contents, then order whatever issue you like. Barnes & Noble stores usually have the current issue.

The Tea Time Gazette
P.O. Box 40276-1
St. Paul, MN 55104
Web site: www.teatimegazette.com

Read sample articles online.

CLUBS AND SOCIETIES

Cardew Collectors' Club
U.S. collectors may contact Sandy Stephenson at
1-877-9-TEAPOT (1-877-983-2768) or E-mail her at
cardewclub@aol.com. Club members receive a newsletter,
"The Teapot Times."

Carter's Collectors Club
Inquire at www.cartersteapots.com.

The Novelty Teapot Collectors Club
Totally Teapots
Euxton
Chorley, Lancashire PR7 6EY
England
tel.: 44-1257-450366
E-mail: teapot.club&btinternet.com.

Application for membership, which costs $35.00, available at
www.totallyteapots.com/_borders/application.gif. Members
receive a newsletter, "Let's Talk Teapots."

Wedgwood Society of New York
5 Dogwood Court
Glen Head, NY 11545
Web site: www.wsny.org

Publisher of *Ars Ceramica*, the Wedgwood Society's annual
archival journal on the ceramic arts; back issues available for
$15.00 + $2.50 shipping.

CONSERVATORS AND RESTORERS

The American Institute for Conservation (AIC)
1717 K Street NW
Suite 200
Washington, DC 20006
tel.: 202-452-9545
Web site: www.aic-faic.org

MUSEUMS AND PLACES TO VISIT

Tina Carter reminds us that "exhibits or museums may have one or two teapots on display and are well worth the visit." I would add to that my own experience: I didn't feel that I had really and truly come up to speed on teapots until I had acquired a good grasp of tea history and ceramics history. Here is a list of places I visited while writing this book, and places I wish I could have visited.

Canada
The Gardiner Museum of Ceramic Art
111 Queen's Park
Toronto, ON M5S 2C7
Canada

China
China National Tea Museum
Hangzhou Double Peaks Village
Dragon Well Road
Hangzhou, China
tel.: 86-571-8796-4221
E-mail: teamuse@mail.hz.zj.cn

Dedicated to the varieties and distribution of tea in China, various tea utensils used during the old dynasties, tea-drinking habits in different parts of China, tea-related culture, and the scientific and technological aspects of tea-making and processing. The museum also hosts international seminars on tea culture and exchange.

Flagstaff House Museum of Tea Ware
Hong Kong Museum of Art
10 Salisbury Road
Tsim Sha Tsui, Kowloon
Hong Kong

Flagstaff House, formerly the office and residence of the Commander of the British Forces, is now a museum housing the K.S. Lo Collection of Yixing teapots, including late-17th- and early-18th-century European copies. Home of the Yixing teapot of dome shape with six-lobed body, signature: "Gongchun, dated 8th year of Zhengde period" (1513).

Denmark

**Nationalmuseet
(National Museum of
Copenhagen Denmark)**
Frederiksholms Kanal 12
1220 København
Denmark
tel.: 33-13-44-11
Web site: www.natmus.dk

Teapot inventories of the Danish Royal collection from 1656, 1665, and 1674.

France

Musée National des Arts Asiatiques—Guimet
6, place d'Iéna
75116 Paris
France
tel.: 33-1-56-52-53-00
Web site: www.museeguimet.fr

The personal collection of 19th-century East Asian art compiled by Émile Guimet, including the Grandidier Collection (collated 1887–1910) of Yixing teapots. One of the world's finest collections of Asian art.

Musée National de la Céramique
Place de la Manufacture
92310 Sèvres
France
tel.: 33-1-41-14-04-20

Accessible via the Paris Métro (Pont de Sèvres stop), the Ceramic Museum was created by Alexandre Brogniart, the son of the architect of the Paris Stock Exchange, and himself director of the Sèvres Porcelain Factory from 1800 to 1847. Home of a red stoneware teapot made ca. 1700 by Ary de Milde, credited with making the first ceramic teapots in Europe.

Germany

"The Green Vault"
Pozellansammlung
Zwinger, Glockenspielpavillion
01067 Dresden
Germany
tel.: 49-0351-491-4622

The collection of 20,000 objects assembled by Augustus II the Strong, patron of Meissen. Having miraculously survived the Allied bombing in 1945, it was seized and carried en masse to Russia by the retreating Red Army, and returned only in 1958. Contains 80 17th- and 18th- century teapots, including Yixing, European red stoneware, and Chinese and Meissen porcelain.

Great Britain
The Bramah Museum of Tea and Coffee
40 Southwark Street
London SE1 1UN
England
Web site: www.bramahmuseum.co.uk

The world's first museum devoted entirely to the history of tea. Edward Bramah, author of *Novelty Teapots: Five Hundred Years of Art and Design*, displays his collection of teapots, which tells the story of tea from the British perspective.

The British Museum
Great Russell Street
London WC1B 3DG
England
tel.: 44-20-7323-8000
Web site: www.the britishmuseum.ac.uk

Like the Metropolitan Museum in New York, it has an extensive collection of ceramics, including the Franks Collection, originally established 1850–1880.

The Cardew Madhatters' Teapottery
Newton Road
Bovey Tracey
Devon TQ13 3DX
England
tel.: 44-16-2683-2172

Free factory tour; factory shop; paint-your-own-teapot (which they'll fire for you); tearoom. Bring the kids; you won't even notice that it's raining.

The *Cutty Sark*
2 Greenwich Church Street
Greenwich
London SE10 9BG
England
tel.: 44-20-8858-3445

The last of the great tea clippers, the *Cutty Sark* was launched in 1869. It is now laid up in permanent dry dock with a museum of tea and tea history in its hold.

Gladstone Pottery Museum
Uttoexeter Road
Longton
Stoke-on-Trent
ST3 1 PQ
England
tel.: 44-17-8231-9232

Discover the story of the Stoke-on-Trent potteries at Gladstone, the only remaining complete Victorian pottery factory from the days when coal-burning bottle ovens made the world's finest English bone china. A unique working museum that allows visitors to see how 19th-century potters worked.

The Norwich Castle Museum and Art Gallery
Norwich NR1 3JQ
England
tel.: 44-16-0349-3625

Home to the Twinings Teapot Gallery, which displays a selection from the largest collection of British ceramic teapots in the world, from 1700 to the present day.

The Potteries Museum and Art Gallery
Bethesda Street
Hanley
Stoke-on-Trent ST1 3DW
England
tel: 44-17-8223-2323

Home of the world's finest collection of Staffordshire ceramics, with over 5,000 pieces on display. Eighteenth-century earthenwares and stonewares, 19th-century porcelains and bone china, and both individual and studio 20th-century wares. Includes items from the former Minton Museum: an Aesthetic teapot of well-known fame, and a Minton majolica teapot in the form of a Japanese man holding a Noh mask, the spout issuing from its mouth (sometimes called the Minton "Chinaman" teapot), among others.

The Teapottery Ltd. (Home of Eccentric Teapot)
Leyburn Business Park
Leyburn
North Yorkshire DL8 5QA
England
tel.: 44-19-6962-3839
Web site: www.teapottery.co.uk

View skilled craftspersons making eccentric teapots by hand. Watch a video, browse in the teapot shop and tearoom.

The Twinings Shop and Museum
216 The Strand
London WC2R 1AP
England
Web site: www.twinings.com

Twinings has been selling tea here since 1706; their shop is the
oldest dry tea and coffee emporium in the world. There's also a
small museum and mail-order service.

Victoria and Albert Museum
Cromwell Road
South Kensington
London SW7 2RL
England
tel.: 44-20-7942-2000
Web site: www.vam.ac.uk

Both ceramic and silver teapots, including the first teapot made
in England, George Berkeley's silver teapot, presented to the
East India Company in 1670.

United States
Metropolitan Museum of New York
1000 Fifth Avenue at 82nd Street
New York, NY 10028-0198
tel.: 212-535-7710
Web site: www.metmuseum.org

An extensive collection of every kind of ceramic imaginable. A
good place for beginners to learn about the different kinds.

Mills College Art Museum
5000 MacArthur Boulevard
Oakland, CA 94613
tel.: 510-430-2164
Web site: www.mills.edu

According to Tina Carter, the college's museum is home to
several hundred teapots collected by Susan Tollman Mills, wife
of the college founder. The collection is now preserved by the
Alumni Foundation.

Museum of Ceramics
400 East Fifth Street
East Liverpool, OH 43920
tel.: 330-386-6001
Web site: www.ohiohistory.org

Under the aegis of the Ohio Historical Society, the East Liverpool Museum of Ceramics houses an extensive collection of
wares produced by "America's Crockery City."

The New York Public Library
Fifth Avenue and 42nd Street
New York, NY 10018-2788
tel.: (Reference Desk) 212-930-0830
Web site: www.nypl.org

Most books listed in the Bibliography can be found in the New York Public Library, General Research Division (Main Branch). Well worth a visit if you're in New York City. The library CATNYP catalog is online.

Parham Gallery of Fine Arts and Exotic Teapots
2847 Armacost Avenue
Los Angeles, CA 90064
tel.: 310-473-5603

Another of Tina Carter's recommended places to visit.

Peabody Essex Museum
East India Square
Salem, MA 01970-3783
tel.: 978-745-9500
Web site: www.pem.com

A busy port at the height of the China trade, Salem now houses a maritime museum worthy of its history. Qing dynasty works, including Chinese export porcelain, textiles, and decorative arts.

Trenton City Hall
309 College Street
Trenton, TN 38382
tel.: 731-855-2031
Web site: www.teapotcollection.com

The world's largest collection of porcelain *veilleuse-théières* or "nightlight" teapots dated 1750 to 1860. Currently 124 of the 525 teapots donated by Dr. Frederick C. Freed can also be viewed online. Trenton hosts an annual Teapot Festival that begins the second weekend in May and runs for a whole week; for information on upcoming festivals, contact the Gibson County Area Chamber of Commerce, P.O. Box 464, Trenton, TN 38382, or phone 901-855-0973.

Wadsworth Atheneum Museum of Art
600 Main Street
Hartford, CT 06103-2990
tel.: 860-278-2670
Web site: www.wadsworthatheneum.com

Home of the Harold and Wendy Newman Collection of 177 superb *veilleuses-théières*.

Tea For One stacking teapot and cup. Paper label, "Made in China." Unglazed red clay. Available at this writing for $22.00 at T Salon and T Emporium, 1-888-NYCTEAS.

ONLINE RESOURCES

There are thousands of Web sites out there, and I cannot claim to have visited all the teapot sites. But I did visit many, and other more broadly based sites as well. Here are what I consider the most useful ones:

Cracked China

www.crackedchina.co.uk
Gaynor Laight's delightful and informative Web site. Anything and everything you ever wanted to know about porcelain and pottery, with links galore. The name comes from the fact that Laight's mother, an antiques dealer, gave her cracked china to play with when she was small. Laight regrets that she cannot do evaluations.

Replacements, Ltd.

www.replacements.com
Hundreds of teapots in what seems like thousands of designs; in fact Replacements Ltd. claims to offer 6,000 china patterns. A good place to find a teapot originally manufactured as part of a dinner service. Replacements will also help you identify your teapot pattern; see the Web site for instructions.

Sotheby's

www.sothebys.com
Information on ceramics, restoration, and conservation.

Stoke-on-Trent

www.thepotteries.org
Don't miss this Web site, which has a history of every single pottery ever established in Staffordshire, England, including a history of marks used by each. An invaluable resource.

The Teapot Tribune

www.totallyteapots.com

Vince McDonald's all-teapots-all-the-time Web site. A must-visit for any collector of teapots. McDonald also runs the Novelty Teapot Collectors Club (see "Clubs and Societies") and arranges teapot events in England.

Some great Web sites that sell teapots:

www.allteapots.com
www.abitofbritain.com
www.britishtraditionals.com
www.holymtn.com
www.racingteapots.com
www.specialteas.com
www.svtea.com
www.Yixing.com

Some useful manufacturers, commercial, and potters' Web sites:

www.james-sdaler.co.uk
www.Belleek.ie
www.spode.co.uk (Royal Worcester and Spode)
www.royal-crown-derby.co.uk
www.lowestoftporcelain.com
www.andytitcomb.com (lots of teapot links)
www.cardewdesign.com
www.cartersteapots.com
www.garyseymourdesigns.com

TEA AND TEAPOT EMPORIA

TEA: A Magazine hosts a Web site, *www.teamag.com,* which posts a list of tearooms listed by state; Web sites that sell tea and teapots; and every other tea-related link imaginable. Below are my own favorite tea and teapot emporia and Web sites.

All Teapots
P.O. Box 745393
Arvada, CO 80006
tel.: 303-456-5752
Web site: www.allteapots.com

The Web site bills itself as "your single source for fine teapots" and lives up to its billing. The site lists hundreds of pots brought to you by Mark and Karen, who also run the A Bit of Britain Web site. Best times to call: between 7–9 A.M. and 5–7 P.M. Mountain Time (2 hrs earlier than New York). Free shipping on all orders in the Continental U.S.

Bergdorf Goodman
The Vintage Dining Room / The Vintage Tea Shop
7th floor
754 Fifth Avenue
New York, NY 10019-2503
tel.: 212-753-7300

Whether you intend to purchase or windowshop, Bergdorf's offers a stunning collection of antique teapots. It also sells hard-to-find Mariage Frères tea from Paris.

A Bit of Britain
Web site: www.abitofbritain.com
(otherwise same contact info as All Teapots)

Art Deco teapots including Racing Car Ltd. teapots, made from the original Art Deco molds for the Sadler OKT42 racing car, "aeroplane," tank, and steamship; Andy Titcomb teapots; Arthur Wood teapots; Tony Carter teapots—and many more. Sister Web site of All Teapots and also run by Mark and Karen, see above.

British Traditionals
P.O. Box 637
Summerton, SC 29148
tel.: 803-505-6500
Web site: www.britishtraditionals.com

Fine foods and gifts from Great Britain; caters especially to British expatriates longing for a taste of home. Proprietor Andrew Ford offers extremely personable and personalized service. A good source for Brown Betty teapots in several sizes.

Mariage Frères
30, rue du Bourg-Tibourg
Paris
France
tel.: 33-1-42-72-28-11

Entering the front room and store, first opened in 1854, transports visitors to another time and place. Above the shop is the family's charming tea museum, and in the back is the tearoom. Reservations required for lunch or brunch. Not to be missed if you visit Paris.

Samovar Tea Lounge
498 Sanchez Street at 18th Street
San Francisco, CA 94114
tel.: 415-626-4700
Web site: www.samovartea.com

The Samovar Tea Lounge offers a Russian Tea Culture
Service, complete with bubbling samovar and dense,
smoky Russian Caravan tea served with marionberry jam
or honey.

Simpson & Vail
3 Quarry Road
P.O. Box 765
Brookfield, CT 06804
tel.: 1-800-282-8327
Web site: www.svtea.com

Quality teas and coffees since 1929, and a nice selection of
teapots and teawares. To visit the store, see directions on the
Web site.

T Salon & T Emporium
11 East 20th Street
New York, NY 10003
tel.: 212-358-0506; 1-888-NYCTEAS
Web site: www.tsalon.com

Highly recommended for the perfect pot of tea in elegant, calm-
ing surroundings. Miriam Novalle, the proprietor, also sells
teapots, among them Yixing and *tetsubin;* various other
teawares; and an excellent selection of bulk teas. From my con-
versations with her, she appears to know everything there is to
know about tea, and a great deal about teapots, too (she collects them herself).

Tea and Sympathy
110 Greenwich Avenue
New York, NY 10011
tel.: 212-807-8329
Web site: teaandsympathynewyork.com

British expatriates (including the famous) and anglophiles alike
flock here for tea and soul-nourishing food like steak-and-
Guinness pie. Tea is served the British way: It gets stronger the
longer it stews, but nobody minds because it's just like home.
The store next door sells teapots and food expatriates can't live
without (Marmite, Heinz baked beans, and Typhoo tea, among
others).

Teaism
2009 R Street NW
Washington, DC 20009
tel.: 202-667-3827; 1-888-TEAISM
Web site: www.teaism.com

At this writing there are four branches of the fabulous Teaism in downtown Washington, where you can enjoy a pot of tea and a light meal. Teaism also sells teapots, among them Yixing and *tetsubin*.

THE INSTANT EXPERT QUIZ

1. What is an Instant Expert?

2. What is the difference between a teapot and a kettle?

3. Define *functional* versus *novelty*.

4. Name the six kinds of marks.

5. Name four possible problems with marks (why you may not be able to extract the information they are supposed to convey).

6. Are all marks believable? Why or why not?

7. If there are Chinese marks on the bottom of your teapot, what book can you use to try to decipher them?

8. What are the differences among pottery, stoneware, and porcelain?

9. Name two tests for porcelain.

10. Define majolica, faience, and delft.

11. What is crazing?

12. Define *excellent condition*.

13. Define *homework,* as in "Do your homework."

14. What is the difference between a fake and a forgery?

15. How old is the oldest teapot in this book, and who made it and where?

16. What did Marco Polo have to say about tea?

17. What was the first teapot made in England and what date was it made?

18. What kind of teapot is used in a Japanese tea ceremony?

19. What was the problem with soft-paste porcelain teapots made in the 1700s?

20. What is saltglaze?

21. What is transfer printing?

22. How do you make lustre overglaze?

23. When was bone china first manufactured and by whom? Why is it called bone china?

24. What is Rockingham glaze?

25. Who was the duchess of Bedford and with what is she credited?

26. What was the idea behind the S.Y.P.—Simple Yet Perfect—teapot?

27. What is the most famous art deco teapot?

28. What was the idea behind the cube teapot?

29. What distinguishes a craft teapot from a manufactured teapot? Name four things.

30. What kind of teapot should you collect?

Answers

1. An Instant Expert is someone who knows how to ask questions, what questions to ask, how to listen to the answers to those questions, how to organize what he or she finds out—and how to then ask more questions, following up on the new information.

2. A kettle is a vessel for boiling or cooking that can withstand high heat. A teapot is for brewing tea. Ceramic teapots with overhead handles are often called kettles, but a more exact use of terminology would be to call them kettle-*shape*.

3. A teapot that is actually designed to brew tea is considered *functional*. There are, however, teapots no one would ever dream of making tea in, and teapots you couldn't make tea in even if you wanted to—these would be considered *novelties*.

4. The six kinds of marks are:
    stamped on with ink (*backstamp*)
    scratched into the clay by hand (*incised mark*)
    pressed into the clay (*impressed mark*)
    raised in the clay (*raised mark*)
    painted on (*painted mark*)
    stuck on (*paper label*)

5. Four possible problems with marks are:
    backstamps may wear off;
    marks made in the mold may or may not show up on the finished piece;
    incised marks may be illegible;
    stuck-on labels may have been removed.

6. Some marks are forgeries; some are deliberately ambiguous; and some are apocryphal or homage marks.

7. To decipher Chinese marks if you can't read Chinese, see Gerald Davidson's *The Handbook of Marks on Chinese Ceramics*.

8. Pottery is made from a coarser grade of clay and fired at low temperatures. Stoneware is made from clay with fewer impurities than that used for pottery and fired at higher temperatures. Porcelain is made from the purest white kaolin clay and fired at the highest temperatures.

9. Porcelain is *resonant* (it "rings") and *translucent* (you can sort of see through it).

10. Majolica, faience, and delft are considered by many experts to be the same thing: a kind of pottery made of coarse clay and covered with an opaque tin-oxide glaze.

11. Crazing is a network of fine lines, usually caused by extremes of heat or cold—leaving a teapot in the attic or unheated garage for years on end, say, or putting a non-dishwasher-safe item in the dishwasher.

12. A teapot that is in excellent condition has no repairs, cracks, chips, or crazing.

13. *Homework* is whatever you need to do to know what's out there; homework is acquiring the vocabulary you need to talk about the subject you are studying; and homework is keeping up with whatever is current.

14. According to David Battie, "A fake is a genuine object that has been altered in some way, such as adding a decoration or a mark. A forgery is a fresh, deliberate attempt to deceive."

15. The oldest teapot in this book—and the oldest one still extant that I have run across—was made by Gong Chen in China, is dated 1513, and is in the collection of the Flagstaff House Museum of Tea Ware in Hong Kong.

16. Marco Polo did not mention tea, although many people think he did.

17. The first teapot made in England was the silver teapot commissioned by George, Lord Berkeley, as a gift for the Committee of the East India Society in 1670. The teapot is now in the Victoria and Albert Museum in London.

18. The Japanese tea ceremony does not use any kind of teapot. The tea is whipped in bowls, not brewed in pots.

19. Soft-paste porcelain teapots could not withstand boiling water, and many blew up or "flew."

20. Salt thrown into the kiln during firing melts to form a glaze, thus enhancing the hardness of the finished teapot. The harder glaze solved the flying teapot problem.

21. Transfer printing is a process by which paper transfers taken from copper plates are used to print engraved scenes on ceramics.

22. Lustre overglaze is made by adding silver, gold, or bronze to the glaze to produce an opalescent, iridescent finish.

23. Josiah Spode II is credited with inventing bone china some time around 1800. It is so called because animal-bone ash is added to the kaolin-clay-and-petuntse formula for porcelain.

24. Rockingham glaze is a distinctive rich-brown glaze containing manganese and iron. When brushed on and allowed to run, the original glaze produced an attractive, streaky effect. Modern versions are no longer streaky.

25. Anna Maria Stanhope (1783–1857), the duchess of Bedford, was Lady of the Bedchamber to the young Queen Victoria when she first came to the throne. The duchess is credited with inventing afternoon tea.

26. The idea behind the Simple Yet Perfect teapot was to prevent stewing or overbrewing of the tea leaves by tilting the pot to separate the leaves from the infusion.

27. The most famous art deco teapot is the original Sadler pre-1947 Racing Car teapot.

28. The idea behind the cube teapot was to create a pot that would stack well on ocean liners and railroads, and that would not tip over easily.

29. A craft teapot is molded by hand, decorated by hand, fired by hand, and sold by the potter him- or herself.

30. You should collect the kind of teapot you love and want to live with.

APPENDIX

Brewing the Perfect Pot of Tea

The best pots of tea I've ever drunk have been those brewed at T Salon in New York City.

"There are short answers and long answers—even entire books—on how to brew the perfect pot of tea," Miriam Novalle, owner of T Salon, wrote recently. For those disinclined to read entire books, she offered a short answer:

1. Use cold filtered water.

2. Choose the right kind of pot. "Green tea likes a cast-iron pot that retains its heat; traditional black teas, such as Assam, Darjeeling, and Salaam, like small unglazed Yixing clay pots, porcelain pots, or glazed terra-cotta pots," Novalle explains. Glass pots can also be used.

3. Warm the pot with hot water. Let it sit until you're ready to brew the tea.

4. Bring the filtered water to a gentle boil, removing it immediately from the heat.

5. Drain the teapot and add the tea leaves. The leaves can be put directly into the pot, or you can use an infuser. But the infuser must be large enough for the leaves to unfurl properly in the water. "When you add the dried leaves they should fill half the infuser at most," Novalle cautions, "since they easily swell to twice their size." Novalle recommends one level teaspoon of leaves per cup in most cases, a little more if the tea leaves are large or include flowers.

6. Time the brew. Black teas should brew for 3 to 5 minutes, and green teas from 2 (Sencha) to 4 (Chinese green tea).

7. Remove the infuser or decant the tea into a second warmed pot, pouring through a strainer, as soon as it is finished brewing. Otherwise the tea will stew, becoming bitter.

I know many places that serve tea the English way, with the leaves still in the pot. Perhaps the British serve it this way because that's the way they've always served it. Sentiment and nostalgia do, after all, contribute much to the taste of anything. Edward Bramah, an extremely knowledgeable connoisseur of all things tea, has said that orthodox, good-quality leaf tea will not in his opinion become too strong or bitter even if brewed for 10 minutes—although he advises brewing for only 5 minutes and using a timer "to get it right."

Generally speaking, Indian black teas are more amenable to milk than Chinese black teas. I once asked a waiter at T Salon if I should add milk to my Chinese Keemun, as I was tasting it for the first time. "You may if you like," he replied diplomatically. "But it's not screaming for it." If you do add milk, Bramah advises that it be room temperature. Novalle prefers that milk is served warmed. "Do not use skim milk," Bramah stipulates. He also adheres to the time-honored MIF—Milk In First theory; add about one-and-a-half tablespoonfuls into the cup before pouring in the tea.

Novalle is strongly opposed to adding lemon or sugar to your tea. "These are old bad habits," she says. "You wouldn't add lemon juice or sugar to a fine wine. Why should you change the flavor of a beautiful, freshly brewed tea?"

People often ask me what I drink, so I'll tell you. Since trying Keemun, I have found that is the perfect breakfast tea for me, brewed very strong. At lunch I make my own Casablanca blend, using 1 teaspoon gunpowder green tea, 1 teaspoon Assam Dinial, 3 pinches of peppermint leaf, and 16 ounces of water. After brewing the tea for 5 minutes, I decant it into a large 16-ounce mug. (You may find this tea a little strong; feel free to use more water.) Casablanca is delicious hot or cold, but I never add ice; in the summer I brew a pot, decant it, and after the tea has cooled to room temperature, chill it in the fridge.

I buy my teas at T Salon, and my peppermint leaf from Adriana's Caravan, at Grand Central Terminal in New York City. I also like Tazo Awake tea, available at Starbucks, when I'm on the run; I even carry Tazo tea bags in my purse and use them shamelessly in restaurants—although I do of course pay for the restaurant teabag, whatever it may be. When using teabags, don't make the mistake of assuming the tea is ready when it looks ready; be sure you allow time for it to brew, just as you would with leaves. As Stephen Twining said at a lecture in Washington, D.C., recently, "The color releases while the flavor is still yawning and stretching."

All teas are made from the dried leaves of *Camellia sinensis,* the tea plant. (So-called herbal teas are not teas but rather infusions or tisanes, and do not come from the Camellia bush.) The leaves are processed differently to produce green, oolong, or black teas. There are many good books in the Bibliography that tell more about the different kinds of teas than we have room for here, and Web sites listed in the Resource Guide. Basically, the processes have to do with roasting, steaming, and oxidizing the leaves. For some reason, the word *fermentation* has always been used to describe what is really oxidation; tea is not fermented, ever, but the term persists. Green is the least oxidized, oolong partially oxidized, and black the most oxidized.

It's fun to read about tea, but you'll really want to taste it. Serious purveyors of tea sell it in amounts as small as 2 ounces. Take a leap of faith: Buy something exotic and savor it! Or take yourself out to a real afternoon tea somewhere. The *Tea Magazine* Web site has a list of tearooms by state; see the Resource Guide.

Samuel Johnson famously described himself as "a hardened and shameless tea-drinker, who has, for twenty years, diluted his meals with only the infusion of this fascinating plant; whose kettle has scarcely time to cool;

who with tea amuses the evening, with tea solaces the midnight, and, with tea, welcomes the morning."

Somehow I imagine that you might say the same—if you brewed yourself a proper pot of tea, using good quality leaves, filtered water, a timer to get the brew just right, and that wonderful, much-beloved teapot you already undoubtedly own.

Lang, Gordon. *Miller's Pottery and Porcelain Marks*. London: Millers, 1995.

Larson, Ellouise Baker. *American Historical Views on Staffordshire China*. New York: Dover Press, 1975.

Lawrence, Louis. *Hirado: Prince of Porcelains*. Chicago: Art Media Resources, Ltd., 1997.

Lechler, Doris Anderson. *English Toy China*. Marietta, OH: Antique Publications, 1989.

Le Corbeiller, Clare, and Alice Cooney Frelinghuysen. "Chinese Export Porcelain." *Metropolitan Museum of Art Bulletin,* vol. 60, no. 3 (Winter 2003): 3–60.

Lehner, Lois. *Lehner's Encyclopedia of U.S. Marks on Pottery, Porcelain, and Clay*. Paducah, KY: Collector Books, 1988.

Litts, Elyce. *Collector's Encyclopedia of Geisha Girl Porcelain*. Paducah, KY: Collector Books, 1988.

Lo, K.S. *The Stonewares of Yixing: From the Ming Period to the Present Day*. New York: Harper & Row, 1986.

Lovelace, Joyce. "The Ubiquitous Teapot." *American Craft Magazine*. April/May 1994. Available online at *www.ferringallery.com*.

Mason, Mary Willan. "The Case of the Flying Teapots and Others." *Antique Showcase*, October 2000.

McCracken, Jerry. "How to Clean Your Pottery Items." Available online at *www.antiqueresources.com*.

McDaniel, Lynda. "Teapots in the 21st Century." *American Style Magazine*. Spring 2000. Available online at *www.ferringallery.com*.

Milbourn, Maurice and Evelyn. *Understanding Miniature British Pottery and Porcelain 1730–Present Day*. Woodbridge, England: Antique Collectors Club, 1995.

Milgrim, Richard. *Tea Ceramics*. Privately published in Japan. Available from Holy Mountain Trading Company, Fairfax, CA (888-TEA-8008) or *www.holymtn.com*.

Miller, Philip, and Michael Berthoud. *An Anthology of British Teapots*. Bridgnorth, Shropshire: Micawber Publications, 1985.

Miller's Collecting Porcelain. See Sandon, John.

Miller's Pottery and Porcelain Marks. See Lang, Gordon.

Montoya, Maria. "New Teapots Pour on the Style." *USA Today*. January 12, 2001. Available online at *www.ferringallery.com*.

Moonan, Wendy. "Devoted to Chinese Export Ware." *New York Times*. January 24, 2003.

Moore, Jay. "Geisha Girl Porcelain Made in Japan." *Tampa Tribune*. March 15, 1997.

Moore, Jay. "Geisha Girl Porcelain Tea Set Made During the 1920s." *Tampa Tribune*. February 23, 2002.

Mudge, Jean McClure. *Chinese Export Porcelain in North America*. New York: Riverside Book Co., 1986.

The Nanking Cargo: Chinese Export Porcelain and Gold European Glass and Stoneware Recovered by Captain Michael Hatcher from a European Merchant Ship Wrecked in the South China Seas. Amsterdam: Christie's Amsterdam (New York, NY: Christie, Manson & Woods, distributor, 1986).

Naughton, Anita, and Nicola Perry. *Tea and Sympathy: The Life of an English Tea Shop in New York*. New York: Putnam Publishing Group, 2002.

Niles, Bo, and Veronica McNiff. *The New York Book of Tea: Where to Take Tea and Buy Tea and Teaware*. New York: City and Company, 1995.

Okakura, Kakuzo. *The Book of Tea*. North Clarendon, VT: Tuttle Publishing, 1956.

Pandya, Nick. "Jobs and Money: Collector's Item: Going Potty for Novelties." *Guardian* (London). March 22, 2003.

Pearlman, Chee. "From Alessi, a Second Chance to Buy a $50,000 Teapot." *New York Times*. March 27, 2003.

Prisant, Carol. Antiques Roadshow *Primer: The Introductory Guide to Antiques and Collectibles from the Most-Watched Series on PBS*. New York: Workman Publishing, 1999.

Ramsay, John. *American Potters and Pottery*. Boston: Hale, Cushman & Flint, c. 1939. Reprinted in 1976 by Ars Ceramica.

Ramsay, John. "Marks of China annd Pottery." *Hobbies*, July 1949. Excerpted in *Lehner's Encyclopedia of U.S. Marks and Pottery, Porcelain, and Clay*, p. 10.

Ramsey, L.G.G., ed. *The Complete Color Encyclopedia of Antiques*. Compiled by The Connoisseur, London. New York: Hawthorne Books, Inc., 1962. Excerpts available at *www.noteaccess.com*.

Reif, Rita. "Antiques: Porcelain Grows in Value after Two Centuries under the Sea." *New York Times.* May 11, 1986.

Riding, Alan. "Escapism in Sexy, Streamlined Fun: Art Deco's Exuberance Is on Display at the Victoria and Albert." *New York Times,* April 10, 2003.

Rintoul, Robert. "Collecting—American Style." Available at *www.totallyteapots2.com.*

Röntgen, Robert E. *The Book of Meissen.* Exton, PA: Schiffer Publishing Company, 1984.

Röntgen, Robert E. *Marks on German, Bohemian, and Austrian Porcelain: 1710 to the Present.* Exton, PA: Schiffer Publishing Company, 1981.

Rotondo-McCord, Lisa, and Peter James Bufton. *Imari: Japanese Porcelain for European Palaces: From the Freda and Ralph Lupin Collection.* New Orleans: New Orleans Museum of Art, 1997.

Russell, Gloria. "Teapot Exibition an Annual Event." *Springfield Register.* Summer 1999. Available online at *www.ferringallery.com.*

Samovar Vodka Collection of Antique Samovars. Lawrenceburg, IN: Boaka Kompaniya, no date (ca. 1950s).

Sandon, John. *Miller's Collecting Porcelain.* London: Octopus Publishing Group, 2002.

Schiffer, Nancy. *Imari, Satsuma, and Other Japanese Export Ceramics.* Atglen, PA: Schiffer Pub., 2000.

Simpson, Helen. *The London Ritz Book of Afternoon Tea: The Art and Pleasure of Taking Afternoon Tea.* New York: Arbor House Publishing Company, 1986.

Solis-Cohen, Lita. "Designed to Deceive." *Maine Antique Digest,* 1995. Available online at *www.maineantiquedigest.com.*

Sotheby's Concise Encyclopedia of Porcelain. See Battie, David.

Thorncroft, Antony. "Collecting: The Wonders of the Deep." *Financial Times* (London). May 14, 1988.

Tilley, Frank. *Teapots and Tea.* Newport, Mon., England: The Ceramic Book Co., 1957.

Tippett, Paul. *Christie's Collectibles: Teapots.* New York: Little, Brown & Company, 1996.

"Top 100 Collectors in America: Sonny and Gloria Kamm." *Art & Antiques Magazine*. March 2001. Available online at *www.the artoftea.com*.

Tourtillott, Suzanne J.E. *500 Teapots: Contemporary Explorations of a Timeless Design*. New York: Lark Books, 2002.

Towner, Donald C. *Creamware*. London; Boston: Faber and Faber, 1978.

Towner, Donald C. *The Leeds Pottery*. London: Cory, Adams & Mackay, 1963.

Twining, Sam. *My Cup of Tea: The Story of the World's Most Popular Beverage*. Andover, Hampshire: R. Twining and Company Limited, 2002.

Ukers, William H. *All about Tea*. New York: Tea and Coffee Trade Journal Co., 1935. THE history of tea *ne plus ultra*.

Valfré, Patrice. *Yixing: Des Théières pour l'Europe / Yixing: Teapots for Europe*. Poligny, France: Exotic Line, 2000. Don't be put off by the French title and publisher; everything is translated into English.

Whitaker, Jan. *Tea at the Blue Lantern Inn: A Social Craze in America*. New York: St. Martin's Press, 2003.

Williams, Lawrence. *Souvenir China: Keepsakes of a Golden Era*. Paducah, KY: Collector Books, 1998.

Wilson, Duff, and Sheila Farr. "Thesaurus Becomes Synonym for 'Fake': More Gallery Items Checked; None Appear Legit." *Seattle Times*, February 9, 2003.

Yu, Lu. *The Classic of Tea*. Translated and introduced by Francis Ross Carpenter. Boston: Little, Brown, 1974. Libraries may variously list the author as Yu Lu, Lu Yu, or Francis Carpenter.

Glossary

Agateware
Made by combining different-colored clays or by combining together different colors of slip.

Aperture
Opening. Where you pour the water into the teapot.

Apocryphal
Of doubtful authenticity. Used by dealers and museum curators to indicate a Chinese nianhao mark that is unreliable.

Arita
Center of Japanese porcelain production, in Saga Prefecture on the island of Kyushu, the most southerly and westerly of Japan's three major islands.

Aritayaki
Wares made in Arita. Also known as Ko-Imari, because they were shipped from the nearby port of Imari.

Art deco
A pastiche of styles including Tutankhamen's Egypt, pre-Columbian Mexico, Greek mythology, Cubism, Futurism, and Constructivism, made popular at the "Exposition Internationale des Arts Décoratifs et Industriels Modernes" held in Paris in 1925.

Arts and Crafts Movement
A late-19th-century swing in the opposite direction of industrialization and the effects of industrialization on the decorative arts. Craft potters (also called studio potters) molded and decorated wares by hand, operated the kilns themselves, and personally marketed the finished product.

Backstamp
A mark that is stamped on with ink.

Bark
See *Crabstock*.

Bisque
Fired but not glazed. Wedgwood jasperware, for example, is bisque.

Blue and white

Usually refers to Chinese export porcelain painted in blue on a white background, and copies of that style. Called by museums and antiques dealers *underglaze blue*.

Body

1. As in body of the teapot, the part the spout and handle are attached to. 2. When used in reference to clay, body is the composition.

Bohea

Used generically in the late 17th and early 18th century by London tea vendors to mean black tea. From the Chinese *bu'e* ("from the mountains of Fukien.")

Bone china

Kaolin clay, petuntse, and bone ash. Considered porcelain.

Bow handle

The same as kettle handle, stirrup handle, and overhead handle.

Caddy

A container for tea.

Caddy spoon

A short-handled scalloped spoon used to measure tea. The Chinese included a real scallop shell to use as a scoop at the top of every tea shipment to Europe, thus caddy spoons often come in the shape of a scalloped shell. Long-handled caddy spoons date from around 1745.

Canton

Kuangchou, now spelled Guangzhou. Capital of Kwangtung Province, South China, and major port on the Pearl River Delta. Port from which Chinese export porcelain was shipped.

Canton ware

Actually manufactured in Jingdezhen but shipped from Canton. The more common blue-and-white Chinese export porcelain, after 1820 shipped in such numbers it

was called *ballast ware*. Between 1800 and 1860 the
United States was the principal market for this porcelain.

Celadon
Chinese porcelain of pale green or blueish green. Sometimes called *greenware*.

Cha-gama
A relatively large amphora-like vessel without a spout,
from which hot water is dispensed during the Japanese
tea ceremony.

Cha-ji
Japanese tea ceremony with food.

Cha-koshi
Tea strainer (Japan).

Chami
Tea scoop (Japan).

Cha-no-yu
Literally, "hot water for tea." Japanese tea ceremony.

Chasen
Tea whisk (Japan). Used to prepare *matsu-cha,* or powdered tea, for the tea ceremony.

Chawan
Tea bowl (Japan).

Cha-zutsu
Tea caddy (Japan).

China
Originally used to describe porcelain from China, then to
describe any porcelain, finally as a name for a hard,
translucent American ware that lacks resonance and is
not quite porcelain but might as well be. This last is almost always called *fine china.*

China, vitreous
Vitreous refers to glass content. The term is often used
to describe fine china, which is translucent but not resonant (and therefore not porcelain).

China stone
See *Kaolin.*

Chine de commande
Chinese export porcelain made-to-order (special order).

Chinese export porcelain
Porcelain wares made in China for export to other nations.

Chinoiserie
A decorative style evocative of China. John Bedford's definition is best: "*Chinoiserie* represents a nostalgia among Europeans for a perennial never-never land in far distant Cathay, with gowned and sun-shaded Chinamen and Chinaladies on fantastic bridges in gardens full of plum blossom." Bedford elaborates: "*Chinoiserie* has nothing to do with the actual geographical and historical China, or the real taste of the Chinese, which is something quite different."

Chocolate pot
Similar to a teapot but taller and lacking a strainer.

Circa, c., ca.
In Latin, "around" or "near." Used with dates. In antique circles, *circa* usually means ten years either side of the date.

Crabstock, less frequently "bark"
In the form of a tree. Crabstock teapots look like tree stumps. Crabstock spouts and handles look like tree branches. Originally 17th-century Yixing designs, crabstock teapots, spouts, or handles can turn up any time, anywhere, on any teapot since.

Crazing
Hairline cracks in the glaze. Crazing can be caused by temperature extremes, including pouring boiling water into the pot (warming the pot first will prevent this).

Creamware
Eighteenth-century delicate, cream-colored earthenware or stoneware, often saltglazed. Josiah Wedgwood produced the best, named Queensware because Queen Charlotte, wife of King George III, ordered a service of it.

Cup
According to Yu Lu's *The Classic of Tea*, at every brewing, one pint of water should be used to make five cups of

tea; this works out to about a 3.2-ounce cup. Modern teapots usually offer a 6-ounce cup; the capacity of a two-cup pot is generally 12 ounces.

Datability
How certain a date can be attributed to an item. A teapot made to commemorate the coronation of William III and Mary II of England in 1689, for example, would be more datable than a teapot made at the same time period with no markings.

Delft
1. Town in Holland where delftware was originally produced. 2. Delftware.

Delftware
Earthenware glazed with tin-oxide, which is glassy and white, resembling Chinese hard-paste porcelain. Similar wares are called *faience* in France and *majolica* in England.

Dobin
A Japanese teapot, often larger than a kyushu. Most dobin look like conventional Western teapots: round, with an ear-shaped handle opposite the spout.

Earthenware
Coarse clay fired at low temperatures. Also called *pottery*.

Edwardian
King Edward VII of England reigned from 1901 to 1910.

Equipage
Equipment.

Faience
Earthenware glazed with tin-oxide, which is glassy and white, resembling Chinese hard-paste porcelain. Similar wares are called *delft* or *delftware* in Holland and *majolica* in England; the French faience comes from the Italian town of Faenza, an important center of majolica production.

Famille rose
Eighteenth-century Chinese overglaze rose enamel. Called by the Chinese *fencai*, "powder colors." While the

British freely use *famille rose* to describe any ceramics painted in these colors, Americans use it only of Chinese export porcelain.

Famille verte
Eighteenth-century Chinese overglaze polychrome.

Finial
The knob on the teapot lid.

Fine china
According to Lenox China, "A hard, translucent clayware that differs slightly from china in ingredients and manufacturing; the terms ('china' and 'porcelain') can be used interchangeably." Translation: not porcelain, but might as well be.

Fitzhugh
A Chinese-export-porcelain pattern dating from the late 18th century consisting of a central medallion and four surrounding panels depicting flowers, pomegranates, butterflies, and other Chinese motifs, with a repeating border design of more flowers, pomegranates, and butterflies incorporated into a Greek key fret border. Why it's called *Fitzhugh* is a mystery.

Flange
The inside rim of the teapot lid.

Functional
A teapot you can brew tea in. As opposed to *nonfunctional* or sculptural.

Gaiwan
Tea bowl (Chinese).

Georgian
The Georgian period refers to the reigns of Kings George I, II, III, and IV of England, roughly 1714–1830.

Glaze
Vitreous substance used to paint pottery to give it a shiny coating.

Hard-paste
As in porcelain, as opposed to *soft-paste*. The museum designation for wares made of kaolin clay and petuntse, fired at temperatures above 1,400 degrees Celsius. Think of hard-paste as the real thing and soft-paste as the imitation.

Hyson
Green tea drunk by, among others, Dr. Samuel Johnson (1709–1784), who wrote the first comprehensive lexicographic work on the English language. From the Chinese *yu-tsien*, "before the rains."

Imari
Originally a Japanese decorative style combining underglaze blue, overglaze *rouge-de-fer* (iron-red), and gold, painted in a rich brocade. Copied by the Chinese, hence *Chinese Imari*. Imari, considered gaudy and vulgar by some, is often compared unfavorably with Kakiemon.

Jasperware
Unglazed stoneware made popular by Josiah Wedgwood. Jasper itself is a hard, opaque quartz after which this type of pottery was named.

Jingdezhen
Previously spelled Ching-te-Chen. Center of Chinese porcelain production, estimated at the height of the Chinese export trade to have over 3,000 kilns in operation.

Kakiemon
Japanese pattern of light tones of turquoise, green, coral, and yellow painted delicately with lots of white background showing. This ceramic is the opposite of Imari, where every inch is painted and no background shows anywhere. Sakaida Kakiemon, the 17th-century Japanese potter, is credited with developing the delicate enamel designs named in his honor.

Kaolin
Clay, mixed with petuntse, that produces porcelain when fired at temperatures above 1,400 degrees Celsius. Also called *china stone*.

Ko-Imari
Wares made in Arita, Japan. Also known as *Aritayaki*.

Kyushu

1. The most southerly and westerly of Japan's three major islands, where Arita, center of Japanese porcelain production, is located. 2. Japanese teapot with straight handle attached at right angles to spout.

Lustre

Opalescent, iridescent, shiny glaze. Gold, silver, and bronze lustres are made by adding these metals to the glaze. First popularized by Islamic potters of the 9th century. In England the technique came into vogue in the 19th century, made popular by Josiah Wedgwood and Josiah Spode.

Majolica

Earthenware glazed with tin-oxide, which is glassy and white, resembling Chinese hard-paste porcelain. Similar wares are called *faience* in France and *delft* or *delftware* in Holland.

Make-do

A broken teapot that has been repaired to restore function, say, with a silver spout or lid.

Matsu-cha

1. Powdered green tea used in the Japanese tea ceremony to make whipped or whisked tea. 2. Green tea.

Modern

Used by some experts for teapots after 1980. Used by others for 20th century. I use it to mean 20th century.

Mote spoon

Used to skim specks of tea leaf out of tea after you pour it.

Nanking

Chinese export porcelain painted with a geometric lattice and spear-and-post border, and consistently well potted and of aesthetically finer and more delicate quality than Canton ware or ballast ware. Often gilded on rims, spouts, handles, and other areas, Nanking was produced on special order only—i.e., private trade porcelain.

Nianhao

Chinese reign mark. Often unreliable or apocryphal; many render homage to illustrious reigns of yesteryear.

Teapots where the nianhao has been proven reliable are described as "mark and period of."

Nightlight teapot
See *Veilleuse-Théière*.

Nishiki-de
"Brocaded." Japanese style of polychrome overglaze enamel later called *Imari* by Europeans.

Oriental lowestoft
An unfortunate misnomer for what we now call Chinese export porcelain. The term has consistently resisted eradication. Unlearn it as quickly as possible.

Pearlware
Eighteenth-century fine white-glazed earthenware; according to Miller's *Anthology*, "an improved creamware body with a blueish glaze to emphasize the whiteness, developed by Josiah Wedgwood during the late 1770s."

Porcelain
Hard, vitrified, translucent (you can sort of see through it) resonant (it "rings") ceramic, made of kaolin clay and petuntse and fired at temperatures above 1,400 degrees Celsius.

Porcelain, red
A misnomer; red stoneware. When the term was coined, 17th-century Europeans did not understand the difference between stoneware and porcelain.

Pottery
Coarse clay fired at low temperatures. Also called *earthenware*.

Provenance
Provenance means that you can trace the ownership of the teapot; if, say, there were a Sèvres teapot brought to Newport, Rhode Island, by my husband's forebear, Louis Rousmaniere, when he arrived with Rochambeau's army in 1780, and if that teapot were still in the possession of the family, and moreover bore the Rousmaniere family arms, its worth would be enhanced because the prove-

nance would be well-established. (If such a teapot existed, I'd love to have included its picture in this book.)

Qinghua
Blue and white; cobalt blue painted underglaze; underglaze blue.

Queensware
Wedgwood creamware admired by Queen Charlotte, wife of King George III of England.

Red stoneware
Unglazed, brownish-red stoneware. Sometimes used of Yixing teapots.

Redware
Unglazed, brownish-red pottery or stoneware.

Regency
The Prince of Wales, later King George IV, served as regent during George III's madness; early part of the 1800s.

Rose Medallion
A colorful flower-and-figures pattern with a gilded, green-scrolled background. In Europe it's called *Canton*.

Saltglaze
Also called *saltzglatz*. Salt thrown into the kiln during firing enhances the hardness of the finished piece. Produces a slightly pitted or orange-peel texture.

Shoki-Imari
Early Imari. Japanese ceramics from the Arita area made before exports to Europe. Sometimes called Korean-style. Simple underglaze-blue patterns.

Singlo
Used generically in the late 17th and early 18th century by London tea vendors to mean green tea.

Soft-paste
Used to describe porcelain, as opposed to *hard-paste*. See *Hard-paste*.

Stoneware

A ceramic that is harder, more refined, and fired at a higher temperature than pottery, but not as hard, refined, or fired at as high a temperature as porcelain. Some experts consider stoneware pottery. For a more expansive definition, see Chapter 1.

Tea

The Portuguese were the first Europeans to give tea a name, calling it *tcha,* as it was called in Mandarin. Other European nations called it tay, as pronounced in the Cantonese dialect (the Chinese written character is the same for both). All tea is made from leaves from the *Camellia sinensis* bush; herbal preparations are not tea but rather infusions or tisanes.

Tea brick

During Tang times in China, the normal way to manufacture tea was in bricks. Loose-leaf tea did not come into common use until the Yuan dynasty.

Teaism

"In the fifteenth century," wrote Okakura Kakuzo in *The Book of Tea*, "Japan ennobled tea into a religion of estheticism—teaism." The philosophy behind the Japanese tea ceremony.

Teapoy

Small pedestal table, often mahogany, with a lidded compartment for containers of tea and bowls to mix special blends.

Terminal

The end of the teapot handle where it connects with the body.

Terra-cotta

Italian for "cooked earth." Unglazed, brownish-red earthenware. Flowerpots and Mexican pottery are made of terra-cotta.

Tetsubin

Japanese iron teapot-kettle with overhead handle that can be used either to boil water or to brew tea.

Transferware
Ceramics decorated by a process by which paper transfers taken from copper plates were used to print engraved scenes onto ceramics.

Underglaze blue
Blue and white; cobalt blue painted underglaze; called by the Chinese *qinghua*.

Veilleuse-Théière
A teapot that sits on a stand inside of which is a spirit lamp to keep the pot warm. First made in the late 18th century in mainland Europe. Also called *nightlight teapot*.

Victorian
Queen Victoria of England reigned from 1837 to 1901.

Vitrified or Vitreous
Glass-like.

Yixing
Pronounced ee-shing or yee-shing. A town in the Chinese province of Jiangsu, halfway between Shanghai and Nanjing, that gave its name to the stoneware teapots made there. See *Zisha*.

Zisha
Clay used to make Yixing teapots.

RECENT PRICES

For an up-to-the-minute currency conversion, consult the universal currency converter at *www.xe.com*.

American majolica corn design teapot, Griffin Smith & Hall, ca. 1879–1880, $425.00 in 2003.

Anglique English Pump teapot, dripless spout, ca. 1880, $1,600.00 in 2003.

Canton teapot, ca. 1880, Chinese export blue and white, Canton drum shape, $295.00 in 2003.

Chinese export teapot, ca 1780–1800, barrel-shaped porcelain with intertwined ribbon handle, top cover repaired crack (visible) and handle has been reglued to body (barely visible), $375.00 in 2003.

Chinese Imari teapot, ca. 1730, almost identical to one in the Peabody Essex Museum, $995.00 in 2003.

Foley cube teapot, in white with black checkered pattern, ca. 1920, £95.00 ($152.49 at conversion rates at this writing) in 2003.

Georg Jensen tea service including teapot, creamer, sugar, lemon tray, and tea tray, $12,650.00 in 1998.

Georgian silver assembled tea service including coffeepot, argyle teapot, creamer, sugar, lemon tray, and tea tray, $4,720.00 in 1998.

Hall China Red Poppy cube teapot, platinum trimmed, China Specialties Limited Edition [reproduction] $84.99 in 2003.

Hirado teapot, second half of the 19th century, loss of lid finial and other small flaws, $1,500.00 in 2003.

Jena museum teapot, designed in the 1930s by Heinrich Loeffelhardt, modern reproduction by Jenaer Glass Teaware, available at *www.specialteas.com*, $35.00.

Majolica teapot, 19th century, Japanese man on a bridge holding a spirit mask, with an elephant-head spout, $1,430.00 in 1998.

Meissen helmet-shaped teapot, pink rose pattern, ca. 1880–1924, H. 4.5 in., $295.00 in 2003.

Meissen 1880 teapot delicately decorated with flowers and insects, H. 4.75 in., $650.00 in 2003.

Minton Anglique teapot, ca. 1900, $895.00 in 2003.

Minton majolica teapot, in the shape of a blowfish, estimated at $1,000.00 before a Skinner's auction in Boston, gaveled down at $28,000.00 in 1998.

Minton 1878 majolica teapot, fish with seaweed handle, estimated $1,000.00 to $1,500.00, sold at a Skinner's auction in Boston for $32,200.00 in 1998.

Minton majolica teapot, 19th century, Japanese man holding a spirit lamp, $2,970.00 in 1998.

Minton Vulture & Python teapot, sold at Christie's for £46,875.00 ($75,242.50 at conversion rates at this writing) in 2001.

Minton Vulture & Python teapot, modern limited edition of 1,000, copy of the original, £495.00 ($794.56 at conversion rates at this writing) from Royal Doulton at *www.shop.doulton-direct.com* or call 44-1782-404045 during business hours.

Samovar, gold plated, electric, available at *www.specialteas.com* for $545.00. Same samovar but in stainless steel finish, $395.00.

Satsuma hexagonal teapot, late Meiji–early Showa (1905–1930), probably made for the Persian market, $495.00 in 2003.

Sèvres Old Paris Porcelain teapot, Empire style and taste, with a Sèvres mark on the bottom, with portrait busts of Josephine and her mansion on reverse, $1,695.00 in 2003.

S.Y.P. Simple Yet Perfect teapot, blue and white Wedgwood, estimate £150.00–£200.00 ($240.27–$320.36 at conversion rates at this writing) in 2003.

Spode teapot with stand, ca. 1920, $835.00 in 2003.

Rare Staffordshire saltglaze teapot decorated with portrait and inscription of Frederick the Great of Prussia, ca. 1760. $1,900.00 in 2003.

Tetsubin, pre-1900 Meiji period, $495.00 in 2003.

Wedgwood art nouveau blue teapot, $179.95 in 2003.

Wedgwood cube teapot, ivory with floral design and some gold trim, $50.00 in 2003.

Whieldon 1760 Staffordshire creamware teapot, $8,250.00 in 1998.

Miniature Toby-style Dickens Mr Pickwick teapot, Artone (England), $25.00 in 2000.

Miniature orange-lustre elephant teapot made in Japan as part of a tea set, ca. 1932, $25.00 in 2000.

Miniature underglaze blue and white teapot, 3.5 inches high including overhead handle, made in Japan, ca. 1890, $65.00.

Miniature Cardew fish teapot, 2001, 1.75 inches tall, $10.00 in 2003.

Miniature Chinese bone-ivory teapot early 20th century, no chips or cracks, 2 inches high, $135.00 in 2003.

"Tea Cup Teapot" in the style of a 19th century barge teapot, modern, 11.5 inches high with a ten-cup capacity, available at *www.teapottreasures.com* for $51.00 in 2003.

Arthur Wood and Son, 22 oz. Chintz Manor teapot, modern, $54.00 in 2003.

James Sadler Ivy House teapot, two-cup capacity, $34.00 in 2003.

Tony Wood Cat teapot, England, ca. 1960s, $65.00 in 2000.

OKT42 car teapot, modern reproduction made by Racing Teapots Ltd. from the original Sadler mold, available at *www.abitofbritain.com.* for $98.00 in 2003.

Andy Titcomb elephant teapot, available at *www.abitofbritain.com* for $58.00 in 2003.

Tony Carter Toast Rack teapot, available at *www.abitofbritain.com* for $110.00 in 2003.

Hall China stock green auto teapot, modern China Specialties limited edition reproduction, $89.99 in 2003.

Cube teapot, blue calico, Burgess Dorling & Leigh, Stoke-on-Trent, modern , 12 oz. capacity, 3.5 inches tall, $42.00 in 2003.

INDEX

Page numbers in italics refer to illustrations and captions.